Praise for
Opening Doors
An Implementation Template for Cultural Proficiency

"This powerfully insightful and thought-provoking book takes us on a journey to culturally proficient actions. Through a key component of cross-cultural dialogue, complimenting Frasier's concept of participatory parity, Arriaga and Lindsey lead us on a path of change that is both very clear and absolutely necessary."

—**Rosemary Papa**
Professor
Northern Arizona University
Flagstaff, AZ

"A much welcomed guide for any district who has made the commitment to the Cultural Proficiency Journey. I appreciated the templates for educators to challenge our current practices in examining the 'opening and closing of doors' for our students and their families. It really provides the next steps in moving forward through the narratives, activities, and reflections. It keeps those hard conversations moving forward. The authors challenge districts to examine practices that create inequity. I will be using the 'Walking Forward' activity as a next step in our district's journey."

—**Lorie Henderson**
Superintendent of Educational Services and Programming
School District of Mystery Lake
Thompson, Manitoba

"Endeavors toward culturally proficient values are critical in a time where we struggle to answer 'Why can't we close the educational gap?' This book describes the determination of one district to answer this question through systemic professional learning. For districts and universities serious about making a difference in the lives of students, this is a must read."

—**Miriam Ezzani**
Clinical Associate Professor in Educational Leadership
Department of Teacher Education and Administration, University of North Texas
Denton, TX

"The power of action to assure access and equity to open the doors for all students was evident in VUSD's commitment to examine inequities and practices from the administration level to all who serve their students. This book provides inspiration for those institutions that are examining and asking the difficult question of, "Where do we even begin?" The activities provided are invaluable to building those conversations and reflections that will move institutions to widen their cultural lens."

—**Lori Piowlski**
Assistant Professor
Minnesota State University
Mankato, MN

"The authors have provided the most comprehensive blueprint for starting or revamping an institution's program for Cultural Proficiency by allowing one to start with self-understanding before addressing others. Emphasizing that changes happen when leaders use Cultural Proficiency to do their work!"

—Thomas Christie
Multicultural/Community Administrator
Lincoln Public Schools
Lincoln, NE

"*Opening Doors* is an excellent companion text to *Culturally Proficient Leadership*. This text provides a framework for schools and districts to begin to critically examine and actualize changes to move towards a more equitable and inclusive environment. If your school or district is ready to move from 'talking the talk' to 'walking the walk' this text will assist you in your journey."

—Melissa Nixon
Director of Title I
Guilford County Schools
Greensboro, NC

"This book provides an easy to read description of Cultural Proficiency in action. School Leaders will be inspired and understand the urgency of putting a plan into action."

—Cesar Morales
Superintendent
Oxnard School District
Oxnard, CA

"*Opening Doors: An Implementation Template for Cultural Proficiency* is a master piece that provides educators and leaders a roadmap for individual and organizational transformation. The literature is a shining example of transformative leadership at its best! Dr. Arriaga and Dr. Lindsey offer an array of Cultural Proficiency applications, activities, and references as a guide for implementation and practice. It is exuberating to see how Ventura Unified School District brought theory into practice that directly influenced the individual and organizational core values to benefit their students!"

—Joseph M. Domingues
Principal
Santa Maria High School
Santa Maria, CA

"I first met Trudy Arriaga at an International Cultural Proficiency Institute where she introduced me to her concept of Opening Doors and asked us the "Are we who we say we are?" question that she instituted at Ventura Unified School District. I recall at that time realizing how well her concepts fit within the Tools of Cultural Proficiency. Her perspective of Opening Doors and questioning whether or not our words matched our action truly caused me to reflect deeply, and I have since incorporated this perspective into my culturally proficient staff development. Trudy has solidified my belief in Cultural Proficiency as being absolutely necessary for improving our school's organizational culture in a way that will help close the achievement gap. Her book will be at the top of my list as a must read recommendation for all my colleagues at the District Office."

—Peter Flores III
Director of Student Services
Santa Maria Joint Union High School District
Santa Maria, CA

OPENING DOORS

This book is dedicated to the Ventura Unified School District community. It has been an honor and a privilege to be a part of this journey with you as we opened the doors to ensure equity, access, and opportunity for every child and their family. Carry on my friends!

OPENING DOORS

An Implementation Template
for Cultural Proficiency

Trudy T. Arriaga

Randall B. Lindsey

Foreword by David Verdugo

CORWIN

A SAGE Company

FOR INFORMATION:

Corwin
A SAGE Company
2455 Teller Road
Thousand Oaks, California 91320
(800) 233-9936
www.corwin.com

SAGE Publications Ltd.
1 Oliver's Yard
55 City Road
London EC1Y 1SP
United Kingdom

SAGE Publications India Pvt. Ltd.
B 1/I 1 Mohan Cooperative Industrial Area
Mathura Road, New Delhi 110 044
India

SAGE Publications Asia-Pacific Pte. Ltd.
3 Church Street
#10-04 Samsung Hub
Singapore 049483

Program Director: Dan Alpert
Senior Associate Editor:
    Kimberly Greenberg
Editorial Assistant: Katie Crilley
Production Editor: Amy Schroller
Copy Editor: Kimberly Hill
Typesetter: Hurix Systems Pvt. Ltd.
Proofreader: Dennis W. Webb
Indexer: Jean Casalegno
Cover Designer: Scott Van Atta
Marketing Manager: Stephanie Trkay

Printed in the United States of America

Library of Congress Cataloging-in-Publication Data

Names: Arriaga, Trudy T., author. | Lindsey, Randall B., author.

Title: Opening doors : an implementation template for cultural proficiency / Trudy T. Arriaga, Randall B. Lindsey.

Description: Thousand Oaks, California : Corwin, A SAGE Company, 2016. | Includes bibliographical references and index.

Identifiers: LCCN 2015034874 | ISBN 9781483388793 (pbk. : alk. paper)

Subjects: LCSH: Educational equalization—California—Ventura. | Multicultural education—California—Ventura. | School improvement programs—California—Ventura. | Minorities—Education—California—Ventura. | Poor—Education—California—Ventura.

Classification: LCC LC213.23.V46 A77 2016 | DDC 379.2/60979492--dc23 LC record available at http://lccn.loc.gov/2015034874

This book is printed on acid-free paper.

18 19 20 21 10 9 8 7 6 5 4 3

Contents

Foreword

This book comes to us as educators during a critically important time in public education. As various national and state shifts increasingly stratified our approaches to educational reforms an array of strategies asked school leaders such as superintendents, principals, teachers, and even entire communities to embrace change in a systematic manner. Educational leaders and governing boards found their roles redefined along a laundry list of principles and philosophies around accountability, management, data, decision making, monitoring, and of course the investment of millions of dollars attached to initiatives aimed at creating high quality curricula and leading students to academic success. In addition, we witnessed in several large cities and small school districts as well school system leaders and state policy makers embracing several market-based educational reform efforts such as educational transformational and management assistance organizations, charter schools, and coaching and mentoring consultants all designed to exert and/or produce measurable student achievement gains. Often these market-based reforms caused the overhaul of traditional reform strategies once based and developed within respective districts.

While these various and numerous what I might refer to as corporate strategies were being piloted, accepted, and often fully established, the Ventura Unified School District concentrated their focus on a two-tiered self-examination process, which addressed, dismantled, and crafted new critical organizational policies and practices as well as vital educational values and behaviors all designed to embrace assumptions and beliefs that were laser focused on our main and most important national treasure, namely our students.

While more corporate and management-based strategies have become popular and gained momentum, the Ventura Unified School District initiated and focused on Cultural Proficiency as a way to approach the important and critical aspects of schooling. Within shifting trends and professional climates, Ventura Unified School District through a close and prudent examination of changing context decided to anchor itself in the belief that through and with Cultural Proficiency practices we can educate students at high levels. The implications of these Cultural Proficiency examinations ultimately contributed to successful and sustainable changes in the lives of leaders, teachers, students, and community members and their schools within the Ventura Unified School District.

I believe this book, *Opening Doors: An Implication Template for Cultural Proficiency*, challenges all of us in the field of education to think of ourselves as true advocates of action through the lens of how we can "open doors" and hence opportunities for every child regardless of race, poverty, and social inequalities.

No longer is the status quo tolerable. This book makes a compelling and striking argument that we as educators have the responsibility and the privilege of opening doors for all students. It also examines and reflects on the fact that this type of practice and journey requires clear understanding of policies, procedures, and vision that all educators have the capacity to successfully educate students from diverse ethnic, racial, and social economic backgrounds. The book provides and clearly outlines a Cultural Proficiency Continuum whereby educators can review and reflect on how we as educational leaders can describe and define how we serve students. The book speaks to us about a district-wide challenge posed by Superintendent Dr. Trudy Arriaga to each district and site leader to identify practices and procedures within the organization that could truly open doors for all students and thereby transforming, guiding, and leading Ventura Unified School District on a journey toward culturally proficient leadership practices.

For education leaders who truly and authentically desire to make a difference in the lives of students and their communities, *Opening Doors* provides a road map to do so. This book is not only a resource that draws from a Superintendent's personal journey it also is one that delivers a compelling professional account on how leaders can create and expand educational and social transformations for the students they serve. The book ultimately illustrates that students can and will learn when they are provided the correct "escort" to equitable opportunities and successful outcomes during that ever so important educational journey.

Dr. David J. Verdugo, Executive Director
California Association of Latino Superintendents
and Administrators
Retired Superintendent, Paramount (CA)
Unified School District

Acknowledgments

We are grateful to the Ventura Unified School District staff who provided us the story to share so that others may learn from their experiences. This book is in honor of the work that has been done and the work that is still to be discovered and addressed.

For me, Trudy, it has been an absolute honor to work with my esteemed coauthor and friend, Randall B. Lindsey. We have utilized the work of Randy in Ventura Unified for the past decade. To be working at his side as a coauthor has truly confirmed my commitment to ensure that our actions reflect our values as we serve students, families, and staff members. I will forever be grateful to have had the opportunity to learn from Randy's brilliant mind and his golden heart. I greatly appreciate the many educators who shared their framing stories. Their willingness to confront practices of inequity that resulted in locked doors was inspiring, courageous, and meaningful.

For me, Randy, it has been a true pleasure and honor to work with my highly principled superintendent and friend, Trudy T. Arriaga. I knew of Trudy's work before I met her. Ten years ago I had the opportunity to serve as Interim Dean School of Education, California Lutheran University, which is located about 20 minutes from Ventura. Cultural Proficiency was a known process to several CLU colleagues who spoke very highly of this new, exciting superintendent in Ventura. Several of the Ventura educators were enrolled in credential and degree programs at CLU and the message was consistent that the Ventura Unified School District was becoming an increasingly inclusive school district and was not shying away from difficult conversations. Additionally, I had the perspective of a close friend and coauthor, Diana L. Stephens, who was guiding VUSD in its quest to develop culturally proficient school counselors.

I have learned much from Trudy as we have constructed this book. Because of her leadership, educating all children and youth to high levels is being accomplished in Ventura and promises to show the way to others. Trudy is a scholar practitioner who communicates clearly and effectively whether leading a professional learning experience, at a board meeting, with local school personnel, or having lunch in a local restaurant.

A special thank you and acknowledgment to Delores B. Lindsey who been our "critical friend" during the birthing and completion of this project. Delores helped us conceptualize the original proposal and provided valuable content and delivery feedback during the final phases of writing the book. We are most appreciative for you and your gifts.

We deeply appreciate our Corwin colleagues who believe in the significance of our work and found it deserving of publication. Dan Alpert, Program Director, Equity/Diversity and Professional Learning, continues to marvel us with his indefatigable support for all issues of equity and access. We appreciate you so very much, Dan! We are thankful to Cesar Reyes, Editorial Assistant during development, always at the ready to lend support, guidance, and resourcefulness. Thanks go to Kimberly Greenberg, Senior Associate Editor, for keeping us organized and on time so we can do our very best work.

Publisher's Acknowledgments

Corwin gratefully acknowledges the contributions of the following reviewers:

Ayanna Cooper
Education Consultant
Dallas, GA

Zaretta Hammond
Education Consultant
Berkeley, CA

Dr. Melissa Nixon
Director of Title I
Guilford County Schools
Greensboro, NC

Dr. Maria G. Ott
Professor of Clinical Education
USC Rossier School of Education
Los Angeles, CA

About the Authors

Trudy T. Arriaga, EdD, has been privileged to serve as the first female superintendent of the Ventura Unified School District for 14 years. Her journey toward the role of superintendent included bilingual paraeducator, teacher, assistant principal, principal, and director. She is honored to publish her first Corwin book with her esteemed colleague, Dr. Randy Lindsey.

Trudy has focused her life work on the fundamental belief that the educational system has tremendous capability and responsibility to open doors for all students. Her leadership has focused on core values that ensure equity, access, and opportunity for every child and their family. It has been her privilege to ensure that the actions of the organization reflect the stated values of the organization. She has been privileged to not only lead a culturally proficient organization, but to live one.

In April of 2015, the Board of Trustees honored her leadership by naming the VUSD District Office the Trudy Tuttle Arriaga Education Service Center. She is retiring in June of 2015 and will be a full-time Distinguished Educator in Residence in the Graduate School of Education at Cal Lutheran University. She and her husband, Raymundo, raised their family in Ventura and are the proud parents of two adult daughters, Andrea and Daniela, and their precious grandchildren, Rayo Mana and Sofia Anuhea.

Randall B. Lindsey is emeritus professor at California State University, Los Angeles and has a practice centered on educational consulting and issues related to equity and access. Prior to higher education faculty roles, he served as a junior and senior high school history teacher, a district office administrator for school desegregation, and executive director of a nonprofit corporation. All his experiences have been in working with diverse populations and his area of study is the behavior of white people in multicultural settings. It is his belief and experience that too often white people are observers of multicultural issues rather than personally involved with them. He works with colleagues to design and implement programs for and with schools, law enforcement agencies, and community-based organizations to provide access and achievement. One of the crowning achievements of this stage of his career has been working with Trudy Arriaga on the *Opening Doors* manuscript. He and his wife and frequent coauthor, Delores, are enjoying this phase of life as grandparents, as educators, and in support of just causes that extend the promises of democracy throughout society in authentic ways.

Prologue

We chose to open with a prologue because this book combines a narrative and a template for designing and initiating a process of change within a school district guided by clear core values and mission statements. While prologue, introduction, and preface are somewhat interchangeable terms, it is the first-person narrative that makes this book distinctive and, for us, takes on a more literary focus.

For the first-time reader this book describes and applies the Tools of Cultural Proficiency in sufficient detail to fully understand the manner in which the tools are aids in addressing access and achievement issues in our schools. Readers familiar with our work will recognize this book as another application (i.e., "app") of the Tools of Cultural Proficiency. We hold a value that each of our books be free standing, and The Essential Questions document in the Resources section is for you to explore other titles as "apps" of the Tools of Cultural Proficiency.

A distinguishing characteristic of this book is being the first of the Cultural Proficiency books to present a case story based on a school district's transformation from unintentionally participating in practices that marginalized students and their communities to being committed, mindful, and successful in making the education of all students a common priority. This book seamlessly aligns diversity, equity, access, and inclusion with the school districts' primary functions of leadership, assessment practices, instruction, and counseling to support student academic and social success.

The Ventura Unified School District (California) has capitalized on national attention provided by No Child Left Behind (NCLB) and California's Immediate Intervention Underperforming Schools (IIUSP) initiatives to address academic achievement disparities that exist among demographic groups of students. Rather than resist change or take a compliance approach to respond to NCLB and IIUSP, the Ventura Unified School District (VUSD) began a two-tiered self-examination process—the district as an organization and themselves as educators. Their focus was to redesign approaches to educating all children and youth to high levels.

What occurred in VUSD was not a slick, new, externally developed and imposed program. Rather, the district began to address, dismantle, and craft new organizational policies and practices as well as educator values and behaviors to embrace healthy assumptions and beliefs about students. The emergent policies and practices of the school and, concomitantly, the values and beliefs of the educators are grounded in the belief that VUSD students are capable of high academic achievement and that VUSD educators are capable of teaching and leading students to academic and social success.

Cultural Proficiency is an approach focusing on diversity, equity, access, and inclusion and is used by school districts and university preparation programs across the United States and Canada. Culturally proficient learning is distinguished from other diversity and equity approaches in that it is anchored in the belief that a person must clearly understand one's own assumptions, beliefs, and values about people and cultures different from one's self in order to be effective in cross-cultural settings. As such, we focus on important aspects of schooling, such as leadership, instruction, coaching, learning communities, and counseling. We are devoted to contextual issues of poverty, sexual orientation and identity, language acquisition, ableness, and systemic change.

Cultural Proficiency is based in the notion that personal and organizational learning is an *Inside-Out* process (Cross, Bazron, Dennis, & Isaacs, 1989). This book is designed for use as a road map to guide individual and organizational learning based on real-life school experiences not unlike those in your school or district. The Resource section of the book provides opportunities for guided book study by individuals and by learning communities of educators approaching desired change in a systematic manner.

Look Fors

When reading this book, we invite you to be mindful of several components that we encourage you to read and treat as "look fors". Each of the "look fors" are interdependent components of this book presented and arranged to increase your professional learning and, thereby, successful use in your school/district.

- **Tools of Cultural Proficiency**—Descriptions of the four tools in ways that teach, refresh, or deepen your understanding and facility with the tools in your professional context.
- **Activities**—A progression of professional learning opportunities that have been field-tested for professional use in your school/district.
- **Reflection**—Opportunities for you, the reader, to enhance your individual learning in terms of personal and professional core values and behaviors/actions that open and escort students through doors to ensure equitable access and achievement in all phases of the school experience.
- **Professional Dialogic Learning Activity**—Opportunities for deeper conversations for school and district professional learning that analyzes and alters, as necessary, policies and prevalent practices that provide educators with the means for opening and escorting students through doors to equitable opportunities and achievement outcomes throughout their school experiences.

With this introduction to our narrative, you are prepared to meet the characters within their setting of VUSD. The plot and conflicts within this story are not unlike those in many school districts throughout the United States and Canada. The theme of this story, opening doors through culturally proficient practices, is one that we hope more and more districts will adopt and adapt as a way to educate all children and youth to achieve at high levels.

Each of the educators who hold the positions represented in this book provided written consent for their roles and summarized comments to be used. Following are the educator roles you will be reading and thinking about throughout this book. As you read the vignettes, quite naturally you will think about your own role and the roles of your colleagues. This "thinking about your own thinking" is the overall purpose of Cultural Proficiency and is supported throughout the book with inclusion of the reflection and dialogic activities described above.

Resources Section

The Resources section of the book provides useful tools to enhance ongoing learning, a matrix of how to use other Cultural Proficiency titles and a Book Study Guide:

- The Book Study Guide is intended for use in deepening individual understanding of the content and for use in collegial professional learning.
- The matrix lists other Cultural Proficiency books and the essential questions that guided the books' development. The guiding questions may guide your deeper learning and your professional growth as well.

As you will see in the Matrix, 15 books on Cultural Proficiency are now available or in production. Each of the Cultural Proficiency titles has a distinct application of the Tools of Cultural Proficiency and the matrix is organized to inform you of which book(s) may be appropriate for your use. Figure 1, The "Apps of Cultural Proficiency" is a pictorial representation of the Cultural Proficiency books. The original and core book, *Cultural Proficiency: A Manual for School Leaders* now in 3rd edition, presents our most detailed description of the Tools of Cultural Proficiency. The books radiating from the "Manual" also present the basic "Tools" in an applied manner relating to the books' intent (e.g., instruction, coaching).

Figure 1 The "Apps" of Cultural Proficiency

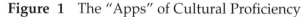

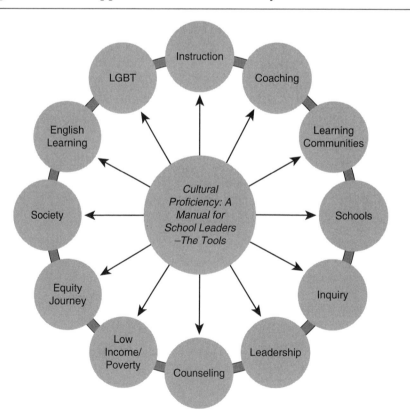

1

What Frames Us,
Defines Us

> . . . it is NOT the diversity that is the problem.
> It is the unconscious handling of diversity that creates
> the lack of fairness in the organization. . . .
> It is that diverse organizations require more sophisti-
> cated leadership, conscious awareness, thought,
> behavior, and tools to reap the benefits of what true
> diversity can provide.
>
> —*Laura Liswood, 2010, xxvii*

Getting Centered—An Inward Look

In picking this book to read, it may be that you are curious about how change was initiated and sustained in the Ventura Unified School District (VUSD). Before reading and thinking about Ventura, we ask you to begin by looking at your role as an educator. We want this book to be a full experience for you and to that end we invite an inward look. Take a few moments to think about the opening quote and the author's description of diversity. Now, think about this question: In what ways do you describe yourself as an educator in the context of diverse student populations? Please use the space below to record your thoughts and questions.

_____

_____

_____

_____

Story of the Ventura Unified School District

Narrowing and closing achievement gaps begins by recognizing that the focus must be on us—educators as learners. When we can honestly say to ourselves and to our colleagues *there is nothing wrong with our students,* we are at that moment prepared to educate our students. When we can honestly say *students' race, ethnicity, gender, special needs, English learning, socioeconomic, sexual orientation or identity, or faith is an asset on which we can build their educational experience,* we are at that moment prepared to educate all students from all demographic groups to levels thought unattainable a generation ago.

This book is the true story of one school district that is a few years into the process of educating students from all demographic groups. The story is one of process. The story is one of heart. The story is one of personal reflection. The story is one of cross-cultural dialogue. The story is one of school leaders holding themselves and others accountable in ways unthinkable a few years ago. The story is one of confronting policies and practices that unknowingly limited students' access to equitable opportunities. This story is not one of unusual bravery and courage; rather, it is a story of educators embracing their personal and professional responsibilities. This story is not finished; in fact the story has only just begun.

We bring you this story because it has a track record that presents roadblocks and barriers to be circumvented and not as reasons to capitulate and not educate our students. This story is about core values. The core values in this story are lived core values, not those mechanistic core values that are too often trotted out to satisfy state or regional accreditation requirements and review teams. This story is about the democracy of a nation that *can be*; it is the modern story of *E Pluribus Unum.* This 1782 phrase, on the seal of the United States, originally described the evolution of thirteen colonies into states of the United States. Today the phrase has evolved into describing the diversity of a country, a diversity to be embraced. Of course, we recognize only too well that the evolution to recognizing and providing for the rights of all people has been one of constant and continuing struggle. This story is how one school district is embracing its diversity and taking its place in a United States that can and does provide access and equitable education to students from all demographic sectors of society.

Trudy's Guiding Question: What Frames Us?

When we, Trudy and Randy, decided to write this book, we thought for a long time about how to begin. I, Trudy the Superintendent of the Ventura (CA) Unified School District at the time, decided to just begin writing and see where it took me. What you see in these opening pages are my thoughts from a frame of reference of having served 35 years as an educator, the last 14 as superintendent. All my years in education have been with this same school district. I begin with the subheading above—a question that has guided my leadership.

Ventura Unified is deep into the process of addressing the reality of the achievement gap with a common focus on confronting educational inequities within our practices and procedures. Early in our journey we recognized that students being categorized and labeled as underachieving implied a deficiency with our students, their families, and too often, their cultures. Instead of embracing deficit thinking, we chose to embrace our roles as educators and to view our students as being underserved and needing to be served differently. This stark realization placed the responsibility on the educator, and we accepted that responsibility with privilege. As we guide all students to reach their full potential, we strive to create culturally relevant learning environments and practices that provide a sense of belonging and support for all students and their families. Over the past decade, we have transformed from unintentionally participating in practices that marginalized students and their communities to being committed and successful in making the education of all students a common priority and a moral imperative.

Where it Began

Our work began 10 years ago as we changed our District Management Team (DMT) to District Leadership Team (DLT) and began to build a foundation of leadership, trust, and confidence among our leaders. In the early years, we touched the surface of difficult issues. We examined the ethics of leadership. We explored the history of our district. We became experts in generational differences. We created and developed a mission, vision, and guiding principles that reflected who and what we wanted to become. We enjoyed team building, *getting to know you* activities, and even learned to laugh at ourselves. We developed deep friendships over time that soon became bonds of solidarity and commitment. We were ready for the challenges of moving our district forward in the best interest of every child. We knew that commitment would take hard work and self-exploration. We knew that our vulnerabilities would be exposed, our unintentional biases challenged, and our comfort levels would be shaken. We were poised to do life-changing work. We were about to begin on a journey of Cultural Proficiency that was deserving of those we were privileged to serve.

Sharing of Stories: Creating Sacred Space

We created what we called *sacred space* where it was safe to share our stories and our life experiences so that we could challenge and prepare ourselves to know and respond to the stories of our students and their families. Four years ago we created the metaphor of *doors opening, doors closing* to help us visualize our actions of serving all students. We utilized our own stories of doors closing and opening to reflect on how we respond to our students. Deep dialogue, vulnerable divulging, and heartfelt reflection became part of the culture of leadership. We realized that we must examine our own stories to determine who we are and where we come from with the realization that our life experiences frame and shape us as educators. Each individual has a story to share and each experience empowers us to gain deeper understandings of our students so that we may unlock the rich potential in every child.

Stories that Framed Leaders in VUSD

The stories that follow are representative of the many stories shared as we recalled and wrote our stories. If you have not done a similar process with your colleagues, it will equip you in responding to the educational needs of your school community. Be prepared to experience deep levels of understanding of self in relation to others, especially those we serve.

Middle school assistant principal

"My parents arrived to this country in the 1970's from Mexico with the hopes and dreams of providing their children with a better

future and the 'American Dream'. Both my parents had little education, but that did not limit their spirits and their will to succeed.
When I was nine, my parents told me I was going to college and
explained that they had opened a college fund account for each of my
siblings and me. That commitment framed who I am. I learned that
the value of education was a commitment of a bank account from
parents who had no money to spare. Today my mission is to be a
mentor and role model. I challenge myself to be the one who promotes and supports students to believe in their abilities and strive for
higher education. I am a bilingual, biliterate, and bicultural leader. I
support our nation as a global leader and I give gratitude to my
roots."

Middle school principal

"When I strayed from the expected path and did what I wanted
to do as a young woman, I began to frame myself as a leader. I trav-
eled alone to nations across the globe to experience the cultures of
others as I learned to experience myself. I learned very simply how
good people are in all corners of the world. People are kind, friendly,
inquisitive, funny, and generous. I learned to give gratitude for my
own story and through my world travels, I continue to learn from and
celebrate the stories of others. I learned to embrace myself as I
embraced the world around me. "

Middle school assistant principal

"It took 20 years of living in a toxic environment to break contact
with my mother and her partner and to free myself from the dysfunc-
tion of family. I became an orphan that day and there was no going
back. When I left, I was told that I would cease to exist. They were
right that I ceased to exist as the person I was, but flourished in the
existence of the person I have become. I found friends who supported
my survival and I believe that I am worthy of the good life I have
built. The abuse is part of my story, but it does not define me. I define
myself. I know that my response to my framing story has provided
hope to hundreds of students in similar situations."

Director Special Education

"I was raised by a deaf mother. I endured stereotypical beliefs
that people held about 'deaf and dumb' individuals. I learned the
power of ridicule by watching my precious mother be embarrassed
by her hearing aids as she tried to hide her deafness from the

world. My mother gave me the qualities that do not require hearing. Her deafness taught me to be accepting of others, to give more than most and to stand up for others, even when no one else is standing. I lost my hearing as a young adult. I am a confident, proud, deaf adult and I decorate my hearing aids for the world to see and admire."

High school principal

"I grew up in a family where no one on either side attended college. I was not a college bound kid. I underperformed in high school and only attended school for athletics. I was programmed to believe that I did not belong in college. My mother left us when I was 13 and I quickly learned to fend for myself. My story has framed me to never underestimate a student and never allow a student to presume that they are not college bound. I am a tenacious optimist. I believe in the potential of every child."

Elementary school principal

"I found myself as a teen parent at the age of 18. I was a high achiever but the pregnancy as a high school senior suddenly changed the image that others had of me. I was no longer the high achiever in the eyes of others. I defied the odds. I proved them wrong. I had my daughter at the age of 18 and I became more responsible than ever before, driven with a sense of purpose and determination. My story has framed me to believe that there are no obstacles too great, that second chances do matter, and that we remain strong and steady in our belief in all students. When they falter, we do not."

Director, Indian Education

"I am a tall, proud, black woman. I stand as proud as my mother stood on the day we were told, 'we don't rent to you people'. My father served in the U.S. Navy and we were told that we did not belong. My story has framed me to be relentless, resilient, and steadfast. I defied every educator whose actions and words screamed that I did not belong! My high school counselor told me I was not college material and my parents would not be able to afford a private institution. A teacher suggested I take the clerical track. I was told that the homecoming court was not for girls who looked like me. I have a doctorate degree. High achievement is for 'my people'. The students I serve are standing beside me as tall and proud leaders."

Assistant Superintendent Business Service

"I grew up in South Central Los Angeles. My reality was continual concern for my safety and well-being. I am the only one in the neighborhood who went to college and became a professional. My friends were murdered, jailed, or became drug addicts. This was my reality. This is the stark reality of many of our students today. I am here to ensure that every student is treated with dignity and respect. I am here to ensure that the stark realities of some of our students are not only recognized but accommodated and understood."

Reflection

Pause for a moment to think about these personal passages. What thoughts and reactions surface for you when reading these brief stories? In what ways were these successful educators framed or defined by their personal stories? What questions arise for you when reading the stories? Take time to reflect on the experiences in your life that framed who you are today. Do you know the stories of your colleagues and the young people you are privileged to teach and guide?

_____

_____

_____

_____

Do We Have the Will and the Vision to Open the Doors?

Now that you have a flavor of our experiences, I will guide you through our thought processes as we continued on our journey to access and equity. In doing so, I am shifting from passive to active voice so you can sense and feel what it may have been like to have been "in the moment" of these internal and dialogic conversations.

From these early discussions that evolved over time, we developed a mission, vision, and set of guiding principles. This book describes our journey in developing "who we strive to be." This book challenges us to ensure that our values do indeed reflect our actions at all times. We speak of our vision proudly; student voices read it at every Board meeting, yet we continue to identify practices that do not reflect our stated values. We understand and embrace the reality that

From My Superintendent's Journal

As we reflect on our own experiences, we create the power to dispute and dialogue about the practices and policies that negatively impact our current students. We may shake our heads in absolute shock and disbelief of what once occurred. Yet, are we willing to confront and address the practices that are currently in place? Are we willing to question the practices that the students of today will someday claim as door openers and closers?

We recall past practices within our district that are often questioned by, "Can you believe we used to do that?" We shake our heads at shocking practices that existed within our district as recent as the 1960s and the 1970s. Can you believe that we use to have smoking rooms for staff members and ashtrays outside the classrooms at our continuation high school? Can you believe that we use to terminate teachers who were pregnant and unmarried? Can you believe that we had girl's lines and boy's lines? Can you believe that we determined how long a boy's hair could be? Can you believe that we incorporated corporal punishment into our discipline policies? Can you believe that gay/lesbian employees could not reveal their sexual identity for fear of reprisal?

We are proud that we can look back in shock and agree that these practices no longer exist in our district. This is not enough. We must continue to question the practices of today and recognize that there are current practices in effect that will shock the educators of tomorrow. Will our students recall practices 20 years from now that closed doors on their future? Will they frame their experiences with, "Can you believe"?

- Can you believe that we employ grading practices that do not accept late work?
- Can you believe that we disallow students into Honors or Advanced Placement classes because of summer work requirements?
- Can you believe that students must have personal resources to participate in many school activities such as athletics, music, clubs, and graduation ceremonies?
- Can you believe that we give assignments that require personal resources in the home?
- Can you believe that we give extra credit for attending community events that require personal resources?
- Can you believe that we hold parent conferences in the afternoon only? Can you believe that we hold picture days, dances, and assemblies on Jewish holidays?
- Can you believe that we have students make mother's day cards, Christmas gifts, and Easter decorations?
- Can you believe that we only allow students to go to a dance with a date?

(Continued)

We are challenged to examine what stories our students will tell. Do we have the will and the vision to open the doors that are closed?

As we examine our mission, vision, and guiding principles, we strive to achieve actions that reflect our values. We ask ourselves if we have the will and the courage to ensure that our actions reflect our stated values and belief systems. As we engage in leading conversations that matter, we have begun the critical process of ensuring that every decision and every action has a lens of opening doors for every child. Practices related to contextual factors of poverty, sexual orientation, language acquisition, culture, and parental access using an inside-out model are explored through real life school and district experiences. As educators we have the responsibility and the privilege of opening doors for all. We strive to update our practices to reflect what we are becoming and not what we used to be. The leverage for change requires clear understanding of policies, procedures, and vision that all educators have the capacity to educate students from diverse ethnic, racial, and socioeconomic backgrounds.

if there is a disconnect between what we say we believe and what we actually do, we must either change the value statement or change the action. Our students deserve nothing less.

We will revisit VUSD's Guiding Principles and Mission Statement in more depth in Chapter 4 and are including them here so you can become acquainted with these statements as early outcomes of our *inside-out approach* to being ever better stewards of our school district.

VUSD Guiding Principles

- We will make decisions in the best interest of students.
- We will value and celebrate diversity and treat all people with dignity and respect.
- We will operate in a fiscally responsible manner.
- We will work as a team.
- We will maintain a working environment that promotes professional growth and excellence.
- We will celebrate and recognize success, creativity, and achievement through a variety of indicators.
- We will embrace families and community as partners in education.

VUSD Mission Statement

The Ventura Unified School District will educate all students in safe, healthy and high performing school. We will . . .

- Inspire all students to excel academically.
- Honor the unique quality and diverse backgrounds of all students,
- Build supportive relationships,
- Guide all students to reach their full potential,
- Motivate all students to successfully pursue their chosen life path, and
- Engage all students to become responsible and contributing members of society.

These are words that are valued and coveted in VUSD. Students at every Board meeting read them and we strive to ensure that our actions reflect our stated values. We have developed our concept of opening doors utilizing the Conceptual Framework of Cultural Proficiency (Stephens & Lindsey, 2011). As we have delved into the process, we have captured the voices of our leaders by sharing our individual stories, assessing our own cultural knowledge, and ultimately challenging our practices and policies at every level.

Reflection

What is your reaction to the "Can You Believe" examples? What questions arise for you? In what ways does this section inform or affirm your current work? Are you able to identify actions within your organization that are disconnected from the value statement? How can we possibly move forward without truly knowing, understanding, and articulating our belief and value system? Please use this space to record your comments.

_____

_____

_____

_____

Door Closers and Openers

Doors closing or opening is the metaphor currently being used in VUSD by educators to describe and define how we serve our students. All schools have doors; some are on hinges, whereas others exist in our values, language, policies, and practices. Whether the doors are tangible or intangible they serve the same functions, either as barriers or passageways. The *Cultural Proficiency Continuum*, which is presented in greater depth in Chapter 2, provides a spectrum of behaviors and responses used by educators and is presented here as an introduction to the most visible of the Tools of Cultural Proficiency.

Cultural Proficiency—Is the door wide open, and are we escorting students through the door? To what extent are we advocating for students and their communities?

Cultural Competence—Is the door wide open? To what extent are we using students' cultures as assets in our instructional programs?

Cultural Precompetence—Is the door cracked open? To what extent do we have the courage to examine access and achievement data to assess areas of discrepancy and disproportionality?

Cultural Blindness—Door? What door? In what ways do we ignore or render invisible the diverse communities in our school attendance area?

Cultural Incapacity—Is this the door you are to be using? In what ways do we send messages that our school is not inclusive?

Cultural Destructiveness—Is the door slammed shut? In what ways do we exclude or marginalize students and their cultures?

As we created a safe environment for sharing, site and district leaders began to divulge their door closing experiences in their own educational lives. The metaphor of "door closers" and "door openers" began to take a life of its own.

Door Closers

The power of words, consequences, and expectations has a lasting impact on students. The leaders of VUSD were challenged to retrieve memories of times when educators used or misused powers to their detriment. As leaders shared their experiences, we once again gasped in disbelief, cried, and even laughed at the absurdity of the door closing actions. We challenged ourselves to think about today as we reflected on yesterday:

High school Latino principal with a doctorate in education shares the story of being in eighth grade and having the social studies teacher assure him that he was not to worry about passing the class because he would be an orange picker like his father.

Assistant superintendent recalled the time a social studies teacher called her a communist for expressing views that did not meet the mold of the teacher's belief and value system. She never spoke up again in social studies.

High school assistant principal was released from the Associated Student Body (ASB) due to the fact that her single mother could not afford the ASB sweater that was voted by all members to purchase. She shares the story of how she publicly voted, "yes" to purchase the sweaters and later spoke privately with the teacher to explain that she could not afford the sweater. The teacher told her she should have voted "no" and released her from the leadership class.

Elementary principal recalls being told that on the first day of class that only half of the class would pass the Algebra II/Trig class. This served to be a self-fulfilling prophecy because he was one of the predicted casualties.

Grant coordinator was told in fourth grade that she would never be a great reader and there was nothing that could be done. That same year, she found a way to compensate for her predicated lack of literacy and earned the class clown award.

The power of words to hurt and marginalize students is evident when presented as we have here. Similarly, the power of words to heal, to include, and to promote are powerful in their own ways. Being mindful of what is said and attentive to the effect on others is an ethically responsible act on the part of educators when working with diverse communities where access and equity issues are of concern. Opening doors cannot be taken for granted; it must be intentional.

Door Openers

We recognize that we are equally moved and framed by the doors that were opened in our past. We reflect on those who mentored, those who cared, and those who mattered. As we participated in recollecting who was "around our table" in our formative years, we shared stories of long ago, reflecting on words that were said, glances that were meaningful, and actions that changed our lives.

Middle school principal was placed in a low-level math class. A counselor took note of his potential and called him into her office. He insisted that his placement was fine but arrived on Monday to find that she had changed him to a college prep math class. He excelled and continued on that track throughout his high school career.

Assistant superintendent was cut from the basketball team on a Friday. He recognized that basketball was his only ticket to success and staying off the streets so he returned on Monday to practice. The coach recognized that he was back after being cut from the team but did not say a word. He stayed and within 3 years became a star basketball player on the varsity team. The coach opened the door for the kid who was cut from the team.

High school assistant principal's family was poor and she was embarrassed to receive free lunch. She pretended to give money to the cashier one day and the cashier reciprocated by accepting her pretend money with grace and privacy. For years, they had a ritual of exchanging money when there was no money in the hand. She eventually learned to be proud of her family status but never forgot the cashier who responded when she needed the door cracked open.

Superintendent was thrilled to find that her favorite teacher, who always taught fourth grade was teaching sixth grade and she had him again. When she questioned his reason for changing grade levels after all these years, he responded that he changed so he could have her as a student one more time. She believed him for years and believed that he liked her so much that he would make a career change for her. Children deserve to know that a teacher loves having them in class.

These stories of Door Closers and Door Openers have one thing in common. Each of these folks became successful adults. Our question came to be, *how many of our classmates were permanently shut out? In what ways do we shut today's kids out so they are permanently sidelined from successful careers and lives? How many of our students are not successful due to missed opportunities because someone closed the door before they could even unlock it?*

Creating Door Openers as Result of Our Work

We began to challenge ourselves to intentionally respond to our question: *Do our actions reflect our values?* The superintendent challenged every district and site leader to identify practices and procedures within the organization that were door closers and to intentionally open the door. Practices and decisions throughout the district began to shift. When difficult decisions were to be made, we asked ourselves if the decision was a door closer or a door opener. We challenged ourselves to crack the doors open and to strive to escort our students and families through the doors. Door opening was included in the principals' goals and objectives and became a part of their evaluation. Each leader was challenged to intentionally identify new practices, procedures, and policies that opened the doors that were closed and widen those that were open. These are a few examples of intentional practices that emerged:

- English as Second Language (ESL) and Adult classes no longer charged a fee.
- Prom venues were changed so that all students could attend. Students could come as singles, in groups, with dates, without dates.
- Advancement Via Individual Determination (AVID) was implemented schoolwide.
- The continuation high school offered courses into the late afternoon rather than an early out dismissal.
- The high school library and computers were open until evening hours.
- Childcare and transportation were offered at Back to School nights.
- Parent conferences were held in the evenings to accommodate working parents.
- Expanded awards at the middle school level to include integrity, grit, and kindness.
- Increased flexibility in the promotion ceremonies to ensure that behavior was not a criterion to attend promotion ceremonies.
- All students were given poster board and supplies to create their campaign materials for student council elections.
- Changed fundraisers so as not to isolate families and out price them from participating.
- Changed policy to no longer return students back to their home schools when exited from special education.

- Offered preschool classes utilizing Spanish as the primary language of instruction.
- Purchased caps and gowns for seniors.

Going Deeper

This final section of the chapter provides reflection opportunity as you read for your own professional experience and growth in serving the needs of diverse student populations. You and your colleagues are provided a professional dialogic learning opportunity as you continue to work for the ongoing improvement of your school/district's efforts in narrowing and closing achievement gaps.

Reflection

Now that you have read the first part of our journey in Ventura, you may be thinking about your role as an educator and the extent to which you, your school, and your district is inclusive of diverse student populations. You may be thinking about particular students or even particular colleagues. What questions arise for you that you hope are addressed in this book? Please use the space below to record your thinking.

_____

_____

_____

_____

Professional Dialogic Learning Activity

To what extent are you knowledgeable about your school/district's efforts to narrow and close access and achievement gaps? To what extent does your school and district engage in opening and closing doors? What might be some specific door opening/door closing activities in your district/school? What questions about your school or district does your reading thus far prompt? The space below is for you to record the thinking of you and your colleagues.

_____

_____

_____

_____

In Chapter 2 you will learn, or review, the Tools of Cultural Proficiency. The tools are presented through a leadership lens. As you read Chapter 2, give yourself time to absorb the manner in which the tools are interrelated and the manner in which destructive and constructive personal and organizational values are made explicit in our and our schools' actions.

2

Culturally Proficient District Leadership Fosters Transformative Change

Leadership is now the ability to step outside the
culture that created the leader and to start
evolutionary changes that are more adaptive. This
ability to perceive the limitations of one's own culture
and to develop the culture adaptively is the essence
and ultimate challenge of leadership.

—Schein, 2004, p.1–2

Getting Centered

Think of your school or school district and consider the following
questions. To what extent are you confident that teachers assign
student achievement grades in ways that are accurate, meaningful,
equitable, and supportive of all students? Assuming improvement in
authentic grading to be necessary and desirable, what leadership

steps would need be initiated? Please use this space to record your thinking and questions.

_____

_____

_____

_____

This chapter describes culturally proficient leadership centered in a moral purpose that schools and schooling can be successful places for students when doors are opened, not closed to children and youth. In these schools students are valued because of their cultural memberships and not in spite of them. As you will read in this book, effectively leading in today's schools is embraced as a rewarding experience for all school leaders: the superintendent, the district's formal and nonformal leaders, and the many leaders found in the diverse community served by the district.

Culturally Proficient Leadership Is Transformative

Culturally proficient leadership is characterized by core values embedded in the *policies and practices* of an organization, or the *values and behaviors* of an individual, which enable that organization or person to interact effectively with one's clients, colleagues, and community. Culturally proficient leaders use the essential elements of cultural competence as personal and organizational standards for assessing culture, valuing diversity, managing the dynamics of difference, adapting to diversity, and institutionalizing cultural knowledge in a culturally diverse environment. Cultural Proficiency is a way of being reflected in the way an organization treats its employees, its clients, and its community (Lindsey, Nuri Robins, & Terrell, 2009; Terrell & Lindsey, 2009).

Shields (2010) describes three types of leadership as a progression of ever deepening change processes. Each leadership type is necessary and is to be embraced with mindful intent:

> *Transactional leadership* involves a reciprocal interaction in which the intention is for agreement where both parties benefit from the decision. For example, a decision in which faculty and

principal agree to twice-monthly meetings that focus on improving literacy skills for all students is transactional leading.

Transformational leadership focuses on improving organizational effectiveness. Continuing with the example of improving student literacy, faculty agrees with principal to engage in professional development for instructional improvement that focuses on literacy literature and skill development.

Transformative leadership recognizes that gaps in student literacy are found in inequities that are generational and correlated with students' demographic groupings. Continuing with the literacy examples, faculty and principals collaboratively challenge practices that marginalize students and press for equitable academic access and outcomes (Lindsey, Kearney, Estrada, Terrell, & Lindsey, 2015).

Culturally proficient leaders lead by example through engaging selves and colleagues in deliberate and meaningful reflection and dialogue. Communication techniques of reflection and dialogue are effective to the extent their use is highly valued and serve as mechanisms for surfacing, identifying, and addressing personal and institutional barriers to student access and achievement. When led, modeled, employed, and used with fidelity by school leaders, reflection and dialogue can lead to powerful and constructive change benefitting all students, in particular those not well served by past policies and practices. The journey of reflection and dialogue when applied to the Tools of Cultural Proficiency always begins with an internal focus. Said another way, individuals introspect on their values and beliefs about cultural groups while schools/districts closely examine their policies and practices as they serve the cultural groups in their communities.

The "Inside" Journey Begins With Our Questions

Valuing students in all their diversity is incorporated naturally in culturally proficient leaders' values and behaviors as well as in their district's policies and practices. Culturally proficient values, beliefs, policies, and practices are intended to achieve equitable outcomes for all students in your school or district (Terrell & Lindsey, 2009). We invite you to ask the important *why* questions and, as Fullan (2003) warned, don't get lost in the *how to* questions (p. 61).

From My Superintendent's Journal

I always want to know *Why?* and I know these *Why?* questions sometimes make people in the organization uncomfortable. I ask them anyway so that we can get closer to our own issues and how we can better serve our students. Culturally proficient leaders pose questions that might disturb complacency toward issues arising out of inequity in the district and its schools. Curiosity is piqued and explored when posing questions such as the following:

- Why do achievement gaps persist among racial, ethnic, and gender demographic groups of students?
- Why are African American and Latino students overrepresented in special education?
- Why are African American and Latino students underrepresented in honors and advanced placement course and in International Baccalaureate programs?
- Why are African American and Latino students suspended and expelled at rates that far exceed their proportion of the school population?
- Why are African American and Latino students underrepresented in school activities such as cheerleading, orchestra, drama and athletics?

Ventura Unified School District (VUSD) leaders pose questions such as those above in ways that challenge them and their colleagues to explore school-based factors that either open or close doors to student access and achievement. Cross, Bazron, Dennis, and Isaacs (1989) in their highly influential work on cultural competence identified this sense of openness to curiosity as an *inside-out process* of reflection and dialogue basic to educators' personal and schools' institutional change. VUSD leaders recognize and embrace community socioeconomics, and they acknowledge the pressures of accountability measures are too often based in political contexts with seemingly little awareness of student learning and progress. VUSD's school leaders are guided by a belief that their students deserve high quality education and that they and their colleagues have the capacity to learn how to educate their students—all their students. VUSD leaders and their colleagues believe that the students who are not successful have not failed the system, the system has failed them. It is the responsibility of the educators and the educational system to ensure that every child reaches his/her full potential. Their vision, mission, and value statements demand this of them.

As stated earlier and often, VUSD leaders believe strongly that culturally proficient school leaders know how to work with formal and nonformal leaders in schools across school districts. At the formal level, district- and site-level administrative leaders embrace their primary function as exerting moral leadership at district and school levels. Formal leaders value nonformal leadership at school and classroom levels by supporting teachers' and staff members' ongoing Cultural Proficiency learning supported by appropriate ongoing coaching. The journey to establishing a culturally proficient school begins with formal leaders closely examining and questioning internal polices, practices and procedures to ensure their alignment in ways that students and community members are afforded equitable access to all areas of the curriculum.

Culturally Proficient Leaders Ask *Why?*

Educators either opening or closing doors to student access and achievement represent diametrically opposite systemic cultures that permeate schools' educational processes in very different ways. Closing doors to student access and achievement is evident in deficit-based approaches to education mired in lowered expectations of students from cultural or socioeconomic groups that have historically underperformed when compared to their middle-class counterparts.

In contrast, opening doors to student access means being mindful of and embracing the demographic composition of the students, staff, and community because of the diverse voices and perspectives they bring to the schooling experiences. Student's cultural experiences are valued and viewed as assets rather than deficit experiences. District leaders are comprised of diverse, formal, and nonformal decision makers. When clear, inclusive decision-making processes are in place, curricula and long-range assessment processes can proactively serve to monitor and ensure that all student outcomes measures focus on narrowing and closing access and achievement gaps. Curricular, instruction, and assessment processes are inquiry-driven to ensure that school and district policies and practices are implemented and monitored to diminish and eliminate disproportional representation by race, ethnicity, gender, or social class over time.

The Tools of Cultural Proficiency enable educational leaders to respond effectively in cross-cultural environments by using a powerful set of interrelated tools to guide personal and organizational change (Lindsey et. al., 2009). Through identifying personal and institutional barriers to access and achievement and committing to lived core values for access and equity, culturally proficient leaders take actions that invite in all students and ensure their academic success. The tools for culturally proficient practices allow school leaders to focus on students', their cultural communities', and the schools' assets in ways that overcome barriers to student success.

So, you might ask, *"what is it I can do that embraces students' cultures?"* It is a fair question that is not asked often enough. First, you have begun this journey in the most effective manner—you started by asking "what is it *I* can do . . .?" This is not an inconsequential beginning. This is an initial step in using the *inside-out approach* to addressing access and equity disparities. This journey begins with the single step of acknowledging what is it *I* can do, then moving to what is it *we* can do. This journey bypasses the *blame game* and focuses on the many skills effective educators, and our institutions, bring to bear on student access and achievement. Effective school leaders know how to pose questions to guide their own and their colleagues' actions.

As educators we have become complacent, maybe due to the pressures of the accountability movements of recent years, in too often restricting ourselves to the mechanistic *What?* and *How?* questions. Sinek (2009) describes the relationship among three key leadership questions:

- *What?*
- *How?* and
- *Why?*

These three questions when used mindfully are designed to foster understanding the power of unrecognized, unexamined assumptions. Skillful use of these questions is fundamental to developing culturally proficient leadership. Each of the questions has a specific position of importance to reflective and dialogic processes:

- *What?*—this question identifies the result to be accomplished.
- *How?*—this question yields the process to attain the desired result.
- *Why*—this question reveals your purpose, the cause for which you are working.

Cultural Proficiency Framework as Compass and Map

The Cultural Proficiency Framework is displayed in Table 2.1. To most easily understand the Framework, begin by reading from the *bottom* of Table 2.1 and follow the arrows to the top. First, we encourage you to look at Table 2.1 and make sense of it as you read inside the boxes and note the bulleted items. Then, read the instructions below to guide you through the Framework. Take a look at Table 2.1 now. What do you notice?

Now, follow this guided reading of the Framework:

The Framework assembles the four tools so you can experience the manner in which the four tools interact and contrast with one another. So, by beginning at the bottom of Table 2.1, you can distinguish

- The Barriers to Cultural Proficiency at the left bottom of the table. Barriers when not seen or ignored or disregarded become *de facto* core values for educators and their schools. Please note that the barriers are not one of the "Tools," but overcoming these Barriers becomes this Tool. More on that later.
- The Guiding Principles of Cultural Proficiency are nine core values derived from Cross and colleagues (1989) original work applied to education. We do not expect or recommend that educators move toward wholesale adoption of these statements for yourself or your schools. We recommend that you use these core values as a lens through which to examine what you say you value and the extent to which your espoused values align with your actions. Put another way, do you and your school walk the talk?
- Please note the Zone of Ethical Tension located between the barriers and guiding principles. This is that area of discomfort for educators that can be characterized by awareness such as
  o Noting that not all students are being educated in equitable fashion.
  o Noticing that some demographic groups of students are being suspended at rates far higher than their proportion of the school population.
  o Being engaged in conversations about achievement gaps.
  o Seeing that elementary grade levels and secondary level courses are effectively tracked by race, gender, socioeconomics, language proficiency, or some other demographic marker.

- o Listening to your own inner voice that might be saying, *something is wrong; this isn't right.*
- o This is an important and productive pivot point for individuals and for schools. If the tension is repressed, the educator and their school become ineffective in working with all students. When recognized and acknowledged that current practice is not effective, an emerging awareness can lead to productive inquiry that informs professional learning.

- Follow the two arrows that direct your attention up to the continuum. Note how the barriers inform the *unhealthy* language of cultural destructiveness, cultural incapacity, and cultural blindness. In sharp contrast the guiding principles inform the *healthy* language of cultural precompetence, cultural competence, and Cultural Proficiency.

- You can quite easily understand that not recognizing or acknowledging systemic oppression fosters not seeing, or not being able to see, the presence of one's own entitlement or privilege. Let's slow down for a minute and parse those two dynamics, entitlement and privilege. Some of our colleagues actively ignore or choose not be convinced by data of any kind that illustrates access and achievement gaps. Similarly we have colleagues who are plainly oblivious to disparities in access and achievement gaps being correlated with cultural group-ings. In each case, active ignoring and passive obliviousness carries with them the mantle of privilege and entitlement that fosters resistance to change. In reality, active or passive resis-tance to change in ways that affords all students access to higher levels of learning occurs in our schools and serves to foster values, behaviors, policies, and practices characterized as being destructive, incapacitating, or unseen.

- Now, back to "overcoming." The guiding principles function as core values to inform and guide individual educators' values and behaviors and their schools' policies and practices to progress from the initial awareness of precompetence to the demonstrated actions of competence and the advocacy of proficiency. It is these deeply held values that lead to actions that counter the Barriers to Guiding Principles.

- Finally, and as we all know, vision and mission statements and their derived core values are functional only to the extent that they serve as a compass that leads to action. The five essential elements of cultural competence become the planning map for our and our schools' work.

Table 2.1   Conceptual Framework of Cultural Proficiency

The Five Essential Elements of Cultural Competence

Serve as standards for personal, professional values and behaviors as well as organizational policies and practices:

- Assessing Cultural Knowledge of own culture, those in community, and of school.
- Valuing Diversity in all that we portray and say that is apparent to all.
- Managing the Dynamics of Difference in ways that conflict is natural and normal.
- Adapting to Diversity of community as it is and as it evolves and changes.
- Institutionalizing Cultural Knowledge as important to professional learning of all.

Informs

The Cultural Proficiency Continuum portrays people and organizations who possess the knowledge, skills, and moral bearing to distinguish among healthy and unhealthy practices as represented by different worldviews:

One that depicts unhealthy practices:	Differing Worldviews	*One that depicts healthy practices:*
• Cultural Destructiveness • Cultural Incapacity • Cultural Blindness		• Cultural Precompetence • Cultural Competence • Cultural Proficiency

Informs

Informs

Resolving the tension to do what is socially just within our diverse society leads people and organization to view selves in terms Unhealthy and Healthy

Barriers to Cultural Proficiency	E t h i c a l T e n s i o n	**Guiding Principles of Cultural Proficiency**
Serve as personal, professional, and institutional impediments to moral and just service to a diverse society by being: • Resistant to change, • Unaware of the need to adapt, • Not acknowledging systemic oppression, and • Benefiting from a sense of privilege & entitlement.		*Provide a moral framework for conducting one's self and organization in an ethical fashion by believing that:* • Culture is a predominant force in society, • People served in varying degrees by dominant culture, • People have individual and group identities, • Diversity within cultures is vast and significant, • Each cultural group has unique cultural needs, and • The best of both worlds enhances the capacity of all. • The family, as defined by each culture, is the primary system of support in the education of children. • Inherent in cross-cultural interactions are dynamics that must be acknowledged, adjusted to, and accepted.

Table 2.1 arrays the tools of Cultural Proficiency in our mind map that we refer to as the Conceptual Framework of Cultural Proficiency. You can see that the Tools of Cultural Proficiency exist as an interdependent network of values and actions that can guide the development and maintenance of socially just professional values and behaviors and school/district policies and practices. In such an environment students from all demographic groups served by the school/district are educated to high levels.

Reflection

What do you see in the framework? Where do you see yourself? Where do you see your school? Where do you see your district? What questions do you have? What information do you want to gather? Please use these spaces for your writing.

Why? Questions Guide Cultural Proficiency

Sinek's Golden Circle Model (2009) provides *what, how* and *why* questions to aid us in using the Tools of Cultural Proficiency to guide our actions, both as individual educators and as institutions. Though the Tools of Cultural Proficiency are presented as separate entities, in practice they serve to inform and reinforce one another. Effective use of the Tools allows us to distinguish deficit-based thinking and actions from asset-based thinking and actions. At first thought, the notion of holding asset-based thinking as a norm may seem to be quite straightforward. However, it is our experience that deficit-based values and approaches are deeply embedded in educational practices serving "underperforming" students and are rarely examined in ways that uncovers biased assumptions. The Tools of Cultural Proficiency guide our journey in understanding our own values and behaviors and probing the assumptions implicit in our schools' and districts' prevalent policies and practices. The four tools are

- **Overcoming barriers**: Recognizing, acknowledging, and overcoming Barriers to Cultural Proficiency.
- **Guiding principles**: Embracing the Guiding Principles of Cultural Proficiency in developing inclusive core values.

- **Continuum**: Using the Cultural Proficiency Continuum to know where we are.
- **Essential elements**: Using the essential elements of cultural competence/proficiency as a template for professional and institutional actions.

As Sinek's Golden Circle Model is overlaid onto the Tools of Cultural Proficiency, we have three distinct cycles to guide our actions. When first reading Figure 2.1, the Cycles of Interrelatedness: The Tools of Culturally Proficient Leadership, pay particular attention to the manner in which equity and access are surfaced for individuals and their institutions:

- The first cycle, Intention, illustrates the dichotomy of *barriers* versus *guiding principles*. This first cycle is important because it demonstrates competing underlying core values of deficit-based versus asset-based values and approaches.
- The second cycle, Assessment, illustrates the *continuum* that ranges from destructive behavior and policies (e.g., cultural destructiveness, incapacity, and blindness) to constructive behavior and policies (e.g., cultural precompetence, competence, and proficiency). It is at this cycle that the guiding principles are embraced as asset-based core values to inform individual and institutional values and actions embodied in cultural precompetence, competence, and proficiency. Furthermore, educators and schools that function at this part of the continuum develop a keen awareness of and ability to respond to values and behaviors that emanate from the negative side of the continuum.
- The third cycle, Action, is being mindful of overcoming personal and institutional barriers to access and equity then embracing the guiding principles and using the essential elements to serve as standards for assessing and planning behaviors, strategies, policies and practices.

Let's take a moment to apply the cycles presented in Figure 2.1 to your school or district. See if you can visualize you and your school or district in the descriptions.

The Intention cycle provides the opportunity to "see" the natural tension between barriers that function as negative core values and serve as closed doors to student access and achievement and guiding principles of cultural competence and proficiency as core values to embrace students' cultures as assets that open doors to access and achievement. Beginning with Chapter 3, you will be guided through

Figure 2.1 The Cycles of Interrelatedness: The Tools of Culturally
Proficient District Leadership

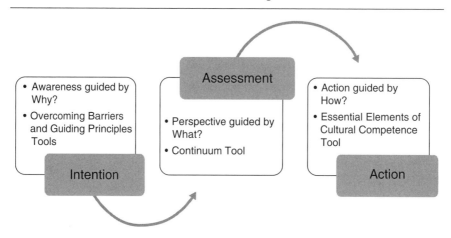

specific activities used in VUSD that engage participants in being able to first see and then overcome often previously unseen barriers. Individuals being involved in deep, personal reflection and alternately in meaningful dialogue with colleagues were able to shift from deficit perspectives by asking significant *Why* questions that explored educators' deeply held assumptions about students. At that point the power of the metaphor of "closing or opening doors" became compelling and necessary. Students and their cultures are no longer viewed through deficit lenses and are embraced as assets on which to build students' learning experiences.

The Assessment cycle derives energy and direction from educators' reflection and dialogue in the Intention cycle through posing *What* questions. The six points of the continuum provides a range of responses from very negative to proactive behaviors that guide participants in actually "seeing" the dominant discourse at their schools about the students they serve. The paradigmatic shift at the midpoint of the continuum, from cultural blindness to cultural precompetence and beyond, is characteristic of individual and institutional shifts from negative values, behaviors, policies, and practices to positive and constructive values, behaviors, policies, and practices. Districts often use needs assessments to determine the following: Are we who we say we are? What data do we need to collect to determine if we are living our mission? What programs are in place that authentically serves all students? What do the data show about which programs (e.g., special education, Gifted and Talented Education, electives, extracurricular, visual and performing arts) serve demographic groups? Once these data are determined, appropriate actions can be taken.

The Action cycle, the essential elements of cultural competence, involve standards for professional and institutional use that employ Sinek's *How* question for developing inclusive values and behaviors and for guiding schools' policies and practices. This cycle identifies educators' behaviors that emerge based on responses to *What* questions. These carefully planned actions are taken based on newly articulated beliefs grounded in assumptions resulting from accurate and informed meaningful access and achievement data about cultural groups served by the school.

It is from our experience with VUSD, and several other districts across Canada and the United States, that a person or school must not necessarily begin at the first cycle and proceed in linear fashion through the other two cycles. We have observed many educators and their schools begin their learning at each of the cycles, depending on prevailing issues in their schools and districts. We have learned that the educators who fully embrace Cultural Proficiency have a deep, often intuitive, understanding of the three cycles and use the Tools of Cultural Proficiency mindfully. In this book, you will become acquainted with the manner in which VUSD uses the Tools of Cultural Proficiency.

Reference Guide for Tools of Cultural Proficiency[1]

The barriers describe for school leaders individual, institutional, and systemic limitations and roadblocks to change. When leaders begin considering the various –isms, such as racism or sexism, they examine their own values and behaviors as well as their school's policies and practices. This self-assessment is often a difficult process for some leaders because they might feel personally blamed for the existence of systemic –isms.

Transcending resistance to acknowledging and being able to name the –isms that exist in their schools is often a twofold process. At the institutional level it begins with an emerging awareness that neither the students nor their parents created the societal conditions that foster inequity. For individual educators, being able to recognize that

---

[1] Authors' Note: For purposes of consistency, material from this section of the chapter is adapted from two earlier works: Raymond D. Terrell & Randall B. Lindsey, *Culturally proficient leadership: Doing what's right for students—all students* (2015) and in Delores B. Lindsey & Randall B. Lindsey, *Cultural proficiency: Why ask why?* (2014).

they did not create the societal conditions that support systemicisms is an important and often liberating first step. The individual educators are now at a pivotal point of discovery. They can throw up their hands and indicate since these are systemic issues, there is nothing they can do. Or, in understanding that they did not create the conditions that foster inequity, they can more clearly see their responsibility, which is to recognize students' capacity to learn, and their capacity to learn how to educate the students. It is at that point that leaders consider more inclusive core values. The Guiding Principles of Cultural Proficiency provide a template for devising these core values and, in doing so, overcoming the barriers to access and equity.

The guiding principles are presented here as reflective questions for school leaders to consider, the responses to which guide their development of core values expressly embracing access and equity for all students. School leaders can use these questions to guide dialogue in their schools, the responses to which can foster inclusive core values that inform vision and mission statements that, in turn, guide policy formulation and inclusive practices throughout the school.

- To what extent do you honor culture as a natural and normal part of the community you serve?
- To what extent do you recognize and understand the differential and historical treatment accorded to those least well served in our schools/communities?
- When working with a person whose culture is different from yours, to what extent do you see the person both as an individual and as a member of a group?
- To what extent do you recognize and value the differences within the cultural communities you serve?
- To what extent do you know and respect the unique needs of cultural groups in the communities you serve?
- To what extent do you know how cultural groups in your community define family and the manner in which family serves as the primary system of support for the students (young members) of the community?
- To what extent do you recognize your role in acknowledging, adjusting to, and accepting cross-cultural interactions a necessary social and communications dynamics?
- To what extent do you recognize and understand the bicultural reality for cultural groups historically not well served in our schools and societies?
- To what extent do you incorporate cultural knowledge into the policies, practices, and procedures of your organization?

The continuum provides the school leader language for identifying and overcoming the barriers of nonproductive policies, practices, and individual behaviors and replacing the barriers with core values that expressly commit to socially just core values. Culturally proficient school leaders develop skills in directing conversation in ways that empower themselves and their colleagues to focus on their responsibilities and opportunities as educators.

The essential elements provide school leaders with five behavioral standards for measuring, and planning for, growth toward Cultural Proficiency—assessing cultural knowledge, valuing diversity, managing the dynamics of difference, adapting to diversity, and institutionalizing cultural knowledge.

Looking Back to Look Forward

Our purpose for this chapter was to look back at the beginning of the journey for VUSD's superintendent and fellow educators and community members. We will continue to tell her story to describe culturally proficient leadership in today's context of schooling. Culturally proficient school leaders achieve excellence with and for children at risk of school failure by intentionally, emphatically, systematically, vigorously, and effectively ensuring students can and will develop to their full potential. Leaders must understand and recognize the importance of addressing diversity in all its cultural, linguistic, and human forms as assets for the school community rather than deficits and problems to be solved.

As a school leader you can only care for the child when you understand what it is like to be part of that child's culture, what it is like to be unable to speak the language of the classroom, or what it is like to go home to a shelter every night. Culturally proficient school leaders connect with children and youth in this empathic way to get to know and better understand the learner's interests and know what they care about, what they do that gives them joy, and what they might wish for if they dared. We invite you to join us as we continue our journey toward culturally proficient leadership practices.

Going Deeper

You now have an introduction and overview of the Ventura story from Chapter 1 and now with Chapter 2 as an introduction and overview of the Tools of Cultural Proficiency. You are well equipped to deepen your knowledge and commitment to educating all students in ways that embrace their cultures as assets on which to build an effective education program.

Reflection

In what ways do you describe your knowledge and investment with issues related to student access and achievement? What more do you want to learn? What assets do you bring to this conversation as an educator, school/district administrator, community leader? Please use the space below to record your thinking.

_____

_____

_____

_____

_____

_____

_____

Dialogic Professional Learning Activity

Thinking about these two chapters, what do you view as the assets possessed in the school/district in moving forward? What do you see as barriers and "speed bumps" to moving forward? What do you want to know and learn? In what ways are the Tools of Cultural Proficiency providing a framework for change? Use the space below to organize your thinking and to record thinking from the group.

_____

_____

_____

_____

_____

_____

_____

In Chapter 3 you begin the journey with our colleagues in the Ventura Unified School District. Chapters 3 through 5 chronicle the sequence of activities we used in VUSD. Though our experiences were spread over three summers with much work being done during the intervening months, your journey may happen more quickly (or slowly). Most importantly, don't short change the reflection and dialogic processes. The processes are very important.

Remember, the disparities in your school, district, and community didn't happen overnight and, therefore, it will take time to unpack old ways of thinking and acting in order to value and behave in inclusive ways.

3

Change Begins With Core Value and Belief Statements

"Weave the cloth tightly . . . so no child
falls through."

—*Arriaga, various times*

Getting Centered—*Trust Us!*

Schools have been discussing, developing, and parsing core values for a while now. Whether in response to accreditation requirements, funding mandates, accountability expectations, and/or because of school or district leadership, your school district has a set of core values. In the space below, please take a few moments and describe your school or district's core values. *Please, don't* pick up your phone, tablet, or phablet and search your district's website. Trust us. Try to do this from memory. Just write using your own words what you believe or think the district's core values to be; accuracy is not important with this activity.

_____

_____

_____

_____

Espoused and Lived Values

This chapter is designed to have you personalize your experiences as an educator, connect those experiences into your work today and tomorrow, and understand and use Cultural Proficiency as a framework for you and your school/district. Let's continue by building on the opening Getting Centered activity.

One can categorize a school district's (or any organization' for that matter) core values into two broad categories—espoused values and lived values. With this book, our intent is to demonstrate how schools can align espoused values—what we _say_ we value—with what we _do,_ expressions of our lived values. An example might be appropriate. It is rare to find school districts that do not express a value for _all students learning to high levels._ Who could (or should) argue with that statement? This is a perfectly reasonable expression coming from organizations tasked with educating children and youth. However, when achievement disparities persist over long periods of time, it seems appropriate to challenge the efficacy of the espoused value by asking questions such as, _why, then, do access and achievement disparities continue to persist?_ In other words, if educators say they value all students learning at high levels, why do the data show that students from some demographic groups are not achieving at high levels?

Of course, life is complex and schools, by definition, are complex groups of people organizing for the purpose of educating students. Therefore, school districts are a collection of individuals with a range of personal experiences that often combine in ways that confront school leaders with competing values. Said differently, school districts are quite normal organizations within a complex society. Educating students who come for a range of backgrounds and experiences and values is challenging work. But, you knew that. That is, in large part, why you elected to be a school leader!

This chapter begins a three-chapter description of the Cultural Proficiency planning and implementation process underway in the Ventura Unified School District (VUSD). Combining what you have learned from the first two chapters with what you already know about schools and how they function, you will discover how the Tools of Cultural Proficiency are situated within an organizational change process. Using the Cultural Proficiency Framework from Chapter 2, we introduce the Dilts' Model of Nested Levels in this chapter as a means to guide the leverage points for initiating change for maximum effect (Dilts, 1990, 1994).

Cautionary Note: Activities Are Not Parlor Games!

You probably noted in the Contents that Chapters 3, 4, and 5 contain numerous activities and strategies for engaging educators in the change process. Yes, of course, you can skip ahead to read and use those activities from this and the following chapters. We advise you to do so only if you have a demonstrated knowledge of the Tools of Cultural Proficiency and a high value for equity and inclusivity that is readily recognized by your peers. These activities are NOT parlor games. Using the activities aligned with socially just values supports equity and inclusion within the context of schooling.

There are two risks, or considerations, as you select a course of action for narrowing and closing access and achievement gaps. Poor planning that is not intentional and heartfelt may result in

- Needed changes that may not happen quickly and, should that be the case, your colleagues may become jaded or disengaged from effective dialogue about equity and inclusion issues in your school; and, sadly,
- Another generation of students will be poorly served.

So, proceed with caution. This work is about being deliberate in order to increase the likelihood of effectiveness.

The processes described in Chapters 3, 4, and 5 are evolutionary processes that introduce and foster cultural changes within a school or school district. When implemented with fidelity, these processes provide the means by which participants examine and often alter deeply held assumptions that serve as barriers to student access to schools' formal and nonformal curriculum. By extension, when educators begin examining their own deeply held assumptions in community, they also begin examining the assumptive bases for policies and practices that impede or restrict student access and achievement. Deep reflection and dialogue are the central processes to surface these deep levels of self-examination. These processes take time.

For these reasons, we issue this caution that these activities are not parlor games. Proceed deliberately, please. Your communities deserve no less.

Reflection

It is still early in the chapter and you may have some questions that you hope are addressed in this chapter or later. What might be some core values in your district that align with your leadership actions? Would a member of your organization know what your core values are by the actions you take? Take a few moments to list your questions and/or related thoughts occurring for you.

_____

_____

_____

_____

The Higher in the District, More Systemic the Change

Change can begin anywhere in a school district but to have systemic change that stands the test of time, considerable reason exists to believe that the higher in the hierarchy of the school district that change is embraced as natural and normal the more likely the change initiative will be embraced throughout the organization (Dilts, 1990, 1994; Fullan, 2011). First, let's talk about what is too common and rarely effective and, then, what is necessary to drive personal and institutional change.

Change initiatives that narrowly focus on the teacher or the principal are no more effective than those that focus narrowly on students' race or levels of parent involvement.

Narrowing and closing achievement gaps directly or indirectly involves confronting issues arising from a lack of response to student and community diversity, which highlighted the role of teacher. The rationale may be understandable, if short sighted. At first glance, it might make sense to focus training suggested by the change initiative to those closest to students. However, what might seem sensible is often met with resistance due to the implied message of teachers being deficient either in their preparation to teach or their inability to relate to students from diverse backgrounds. More cynically, such initiatives communicate that teachers (or principals) bear primary responsibility for student under performance.

The degree of commitment to a systemic change initiative that a school or district holds is often the primary indicator of success or failure in reaching the intended objective. Thoughtful, well-planned change initiatives involve all levels of the school or district and are designed, implemented, and assessed as continuous improvement processes (Hargreaves & Fullan, 2012). The journey of continuous improvement uses data to inform and revise implementation strategies; data are never used as gotchas or to malign any sector of the district. Bateson and Dilts' *Nested Levels of Learning,* as adapted by Garmston and Wellman (1999), serves as a model of behavioral and organizational change.

The Dilts model closely parallels the work under way in VUSD where district leaders began by addressing two key questions regarding identify and beliefs:

- Who are we?
- Why do we do what we do?

The nested level model for implementing and directing change efforts is predicated on the notion that behavioral and observable

Table 3.1   Nested Levels of Organizational Change

Identity: The individual's or group's sense of self Answers the questions: *Who are we?* or *Who am I?*
Belief System: The individual's or group's values, beliefs, assumptions, and meanings Answers the question: *Why do we do what we do?*
Capabilities: The individual's and group's reflective and dialogic skills to use new knowledge, understanding, and skills Answers the question: *How will we develop and use the skills that we have?*
Behaviors: The individual's or group's actions and reactions Answers the question: *In what specific behaviors will I or we engage?*
Environment: Basic physical surroundings, tools, materials, supplies, and technology Answers the question: *What do we need to begin?*

changes most significantly occur when all levels of the school/district are involved. Irrespective of where the change initiative is introduced, the initiative most directly impacts behaviors of colleagues at that level and below that level in the school/district. Therefore, when the change initiative is embraced at the leadership level of the school district priorities are unambiguous; everyone is involved. Change initiatives are intentional, supported, and involve the totality of the district.

Limitations of Change Initiatives Begun Elsewhere in a District

Change initiatives assigned by the superintendent and board of education to school levels may, in fact, produce expected results at a given school; however, they should not be expected to provide systemic changes in a school or district. An example of the limitations of school-level change within a district would be if the Educational Foundation of one elementary school chose to give every student an IPad at their school; that change may or may not impact other schools in the district. Similarly, social studies teachers at the local high school deciding to implement a professional learning community for their department may or may not impact other teachers at the school or even other social studies teachers throughout the district. Accordingly, if a principal at one school in the district decided to implement student-led parent conferences as a change initiative, that change might occur only at that school and have no influence throughout the district, in so doing lessening the chances or opportunities for district-wide, systemic changes.

An illustration is in order here. Let's take the mythical ABC Middle School in the XYZ School District. At the ABC Middle School the administrators and teachers have decided to focus on equity issues related to perceived disproportionate student suspensions of African American and Latino male students. Preliminary examination of suspension data for the last three years reveals this is an issue that has been avoided and, also, not going away. In the event this school embraces a social justice perspective, such as that embedded within Cultural Proficiency, they will ask themselves the questions that appear in Table 3.1. Take a moment, and beginning at the lowest level of the model the higher you ascend in the model the more likely you are to have a sustainable change effort.

Keeping with our ABC Middle School change initiative, assume the educators engage only with questions from the lower rungs: *In what specific behaviors will I or we engage?* Or *What do we need to begin?* As you can imagine, or maybe have experienced, the change initiative will be short term or have limited impact. In terms of addressing disproportionate student suspensions, questions such as these will have educators at ABC thrashing around to locate and implement "can't fail programs" without examining deeper issues that contribute to student, educator, and parent/guardian roles in student access and achievement.

However, if these same educators begin to pose and respond to the higher order questions in the model and begin to peel back assumptions operating in the school that shape educator behavior and school policy regarding disproportionate suspensions, they most likely will be onto something of value. Not only will students benefit from this process, the educators will feel empowered in their new ways of perceiving and valuing their students.

Now let's take our initiative district wide in the XYZ District. The veracity of the model is the same districtwide as it was at the local school level. Asking only questions at the lowest rungs of the model keeps us asking *what* and *how* questions and not the substantive *why* questions. It is when we probe our identity as a school district in ways that reveals and embraces all students that we are able to probe our individual educator and district values, beliefs, and assumptions about our students and our capabilities (Sinek, 2009). Educators make the commitment to self and to the community served by the district when they embrace and value our students as they are, as opposed to whom they used to be or whom we might wish them to be. Engaging in introspection and professional learning informed by *how* questions guides selections in curriculum, instruction, assessment, and parent/community engagement in ways that treats disproportional student suspensions as central to our collective work as educators.

Systemic Change Initiative in Ventura

Educators in VUSD have been engaged in collaborative conversations and data dialogues as part of their district-wide reform efforts to support all students, educators, parents/guardians, and community members. Take a few moments and read Table 3.2—from the top, this time! Take note of the progression from values and beliefs to actions as you move through the table.

Table 3.2   VUSD's Nested Levels and Leverage Points Implementation

Ventura Unified School District Board and Superintendent promote the district identity as high performing academically, with student-centered instruction and community engagement. The result of the District's focus is an inclusive and cohesive district goal and community-wide vision aligned with Common Core State Standards.
Answers the question: *Who are we?*

Superintendent's leadership cabinet hosts conversations/professional learning focused on district-wide mission, core values, belief statements, and public agreements. These agreements are aligned with Board's goals and district vision statement/identity.
Answers the question: *Why do we do what we do?*

District office and site leaders demonstrate high value for professional learning that supports teachers and leaders by providing this book to engage teachers, counselors, administrators, paraprofessionals, parents/guardians, and community members in effective educational practices.
Answers the question: *How will we develop new skills and/or use the skills that we have?*

VUSD educators adopt a well-defined plan of standards-based curriculum, instruction, and assessment aligned with languages, academic needs, and cultural backgrounds of students. Educators engage in comprehensive, culturally proficient, professional learning focused on needs of historically underserved students as well as educators and parents/community members.
Answers the question: *In what specific behaviors will we engage?*

School site educators create supportive conditions, providing facilities, resources, and appropriate materials to engage educators in implementing standards-based curriculum, instruction, and assessment.
Answers the question: *What do we need to begin?*

The Cultural Proficiency Framework combined with the Dilts model of nested levels of behavioral and organizational change provides powerful tools to use as lenses for change initiatives in your school or district. Importantly, these are not additional tasks or things for you do to. The Cultural Proficiency Framework and the Dilts model serve as action guides and benchmarks for designing and implementing change initiatives that push all students' educational access and academic achievement forward.

Reflection

What do you see in the Dilts model? In what ways does the Dilts model inform your work as an educator? As you read Table 3.2 and the VUSD approach, in what ways did this inform your understanding of systemic change as it affects issues of student access and academic achievement? Please use the space below to record your thinking.

_____

_____

_____

_____

From My Superintendent's Journal

I think back to the time when I was a new principal at Sheridan Way Elementary School in the late '80s. I felt privileged to serve the 700 children, their families, and staff members. I noticed within a few weeks that there were aspects of the culture that did not honor all those who walked the halls and it was my responsibility to ensure that our actions reflected our stated values.

Henry Calloway was a dedicated staff member and served as the custodian of our school. He was the only African American male staff member on our campus. I immediately noticed that the children of the school called him exclusively by his first name unlike the last name titles reserved for other adults on campus. I spoke with him about my observation and he assured me that the children had always called him by his first name and this was of no concern to him. I let him know that this practice concerned me as the new principal. Out of respect for him and all those in the school community, I informed the children that Henry was to be called Mr. Calloway in the future. Within a few days, Henry became Mr. Calloway and it never crossed my mind again.

(Continued)

(Continued)

Mr. Calloway retired from our district years later and his retirement party was held in my home. At the end of the party, he took me aside and told me that his greatest day in VUSD was the day he became Mr. Calloway. Mr. Henry Calloway helped me to realize that my leadership could change lives. I also realized that we must continue to examine our policies and procedures because we surely have some "can you believe" practices in our current system today. Activity 3.1 is dedicated to our honorable custodian, Mr. Henry Calloway.

As the superintendent, I knew we were ready to take on the courageous conversations that would result from our two planned activities. The District Leadership Team (DLT) meeting in August, 2012 was not the beginning. We were deep in the middle of Cultural Proficiency because we had spent years creating our values, examining our personal journeys, confronting our biases, trusting our colleagues, and defining Cultural Proficiency.

The day began with a look back in time. Activity 3.1 resulted from a recollection of the '60s through the '80s in our district. Most had not been around during "those days", but I had been in VUSD as a student and a teacher. We laughed at the absurdity of firing an elementary school teacher for being pregnant and unmarried and were shocked to recall that mother/daughter events were commonplace, clearly excluding every female child without a mother in the home.

An experience from 20 years prior resulted in Activity 3.2. I recalled a field trip to Los Angeles' Museum of Tolerance (MOT). I was a young principal at the time and although I appreciated the opportunity to experience such a powerful venue with my colleagues, I was disappointed that it was an isolated experience and did not connect to our practices as leaders in any ongoing fashion.

I have a very vivid memory of one exercise during that visit to the MOT. The activity had us take one step forward if the statement referred to our personal life experiences and to stand still if the statement did not refer to our personal life experiences. There were statements such as, "I can go to a bank and be confident that the president will look like me," and "I can get Band-Aids that are the color of my skin". I recall that the white males in the room walked forward with ease as each statement was made. The white females were not far behind. My colleagues of color were slow to move forward and the very few African Americans in our group stood still. It was a moving exercise and hit a very vulnerable chord within each of us, but in different ways. I remember that a few of my colleagues of color expressed discomfort with the exercise and suggested that they did not appreciate exposing and experiencing discrimination they knew to be true in such fashion. The experience was instructive for some and all too true for others.

That activity stayed with me, and I often thought about attempting it with the DLT but never felt comfortable with the venue as it had been provided. It dawned on me about 10 years ago that the activity could be extremely powerful and eliminate the personal vulnerability if we utilized it to explore our educational system. What if we observed the impact of our system by watching our students walking forward with confidence or slightly moving or standing still? So, I altered the walking forward experience. I asked each site level administrator to provide me with the composition of a random family from their school site. I received 27 descriptions of randomly selected families in VUSD and I selected 7 for use in the experience. With large signs depicting the composition of their families held to the chests of 7 staff members, we proceeded with the activity. The directions were to "move one step forward if the statement is one that your family can easily accomplish. Stand still if your family cannot easily accomplish the task." We were ready, but we were not prepared for the visual and blatant outcome of our students' abilities and inabilities to walk forward within our system. I read statements that pertained to our District. I read common practices that I observed on a daily basis as we watched some families move forward within our system with confidence and ease, while others moved slowly within our system, and yet others never got a foot out of the "door".

We watched in silence as we observed Family #7 take bold steps forward with every statement made about our practices. We felt anguish as we watched Family #6 never take a step. We took note that our system was designed to ensure success for the Caucasian, English speaking, well-educated, financially able, heterosexual family. We realized that the demographics of our district were 50% Free and Reduced Lunch (California's metric for families from low-income and impoverished backgrounds), 25 % English Language Learning Students. We were inviting failure for the majority of our students! At that moment we realized that these are our families and this is our school system. We knew we had to make dramatic changes in the system to provide every family with the ease of walking forward in VUSD. We vowed that year to make intentional changes. Our next steps were very visible and very clear. It was time to tackle our practices that were closing doors. It was time to ensure that all families move forward in VUSD. We felt a sense of urgency and the visualization of the activity served as a constant reminder that our families would not move forward until we took action. We immediately agreed that one of the goals for every principal in the upcoming year was to identify and implement intentional practices to ensure that all children are walking forward.

That afternoon was momentous as we watched some VUSD families walk across the room with ease, while some took a few steps forward, and others never moved. The reason some of the families were not able to move forward was not a result of their deficit it was clearly our deficit.

Continuum as Guide

Creating Initial Awareness Is Cultural Precompetence

We ask you now to use the Cultural Proficiency Framework (Table 2.1) as your reading guide. *Cultural Precompetence* is the point along the continuum where educators become aware that current practices are not serving all students equitably. Several data points used singly or in combination can illustrate inequity:

- Academic achievement gaps in basic skills areas of language arts and mathematics.
- Access gaps among racial, ethnic, gender, and/or language learning students in special education, advanced placement, and/or International Baccalaureate classes and programs.
- Disproportionate suspension and expulsion rates among racial, ethnic, gender, and/or language learning students.
- Disproportionate representation in extracurricular participation among racial, ethnic, gender, and/or language learning students.
- And, the list can be extended.

When educators become aware of disparities and disproportional representation and are willing to begin to examine what they can do as educators within the school community, that is the moment of Cultural Precompetence. The refreshing thing about being at this point of development is recognizing the scope of the problem and expressing a willingness to learn. This is the point of initiating the *inside-out* process of change described in Chapter 2. Paraphrasing the character Tom Hanks played as the astronaut Jim Lovell in Apollo 13, *Houston, we have a problem!* You have to see the problem before you can begin addressing and solving the problem.

Initiating the Template as Lead Learner for Awareness

Successes being experienced by VUSD began by investing time to deeply commit to developing a vision, mission, and guiding principles that unambiguously focus on all students achieving to high academic levels. Too often school district vision and mission statements are rhetorical devices intended to satisfy external accreditation requirements and bear little similarity to what actually occurs at the district office, let alone in the school and classrooms across the district. VUSD is different in that they hold themselves accountable to these pronouncements and the two activities in this chapter were used to begin and to quickly deepen their commitment to access and equity.

The activities are presented in the sequence used in VUSD. Each activity is presented in lesson plan format complete with purpose statements, needed time frames, and suggested sequence of steps. Following each activity is opportunity for you to think about how the activity might be best used in your school or district context. The two activities for this chapter are

- **Can You Believe?**—This activity serves to anchor each participant to understand and reexperience his or her years as a student and to recall practices that served to diminish student participation.
- **Walking Forward Part I**—This activity serves to have participants experience what it is like to be moved forward or backward by prevalent policies and practices in schools.

Activity 3.1—Can You Believe?

Purpose: To create and experience empathy through recalling and sharing practices and procedures implemented in the past years of our lives that closed doors on students. To examine practices of today that are door closers and to initiate conversation of how to change current practices so they will not be the door closers of the future.

Readiness of Group: Beginning

Time Needed: 1–2 hours

Materials: Prepared list of past practices in previous decades in a visual format. (Sample template follows.)

Process

- Begin the discussion with an opportunity for participants to recall past practices in their K–12 years as students that are "unbelievable" today.
- Present the prepared list of past practices in a visual format to heighten the awareness and enhance the recall of the participants. See list provided for possible use or modification.
- If possible, prepare the list of past practices from the school district in which the work is being done. Invite the participants to add practices from their personal recollection.
- Begin to prepare participants for future discussions by challenging participants to change the focus on previous decades and focus on current practices.
- Are there practices in existence today that will be the "can you believes" of future generations of students?

Debriefing

- How did you feel as a child that did not move forward within the procedures of the district?
- How did the audience feel about watching some children stand still?
- Were the procedures common to your site or district?
- Do we need to change the children or change the system? In what ways?

Next Steps

Require every school principal to submit 2–3 new goals that will intentionally address a student's ability to walk forward within the system. Revisit the goals throughout the year and collect them for the Walking Forward Part 2 (Chapter 4) activity to follow within 6 months to a year.

Sample Template for the Activity

Thinking back to your school days in elementary school days, are you able to retrieve actions, decisions, and policies that have changed over the years? Let me take you back to VUSD in the 1950s….1960s…. and early 1970s with some educational practices that are difficult to believe occurred.

- Can you believe that special education students were not in regular education classes?
- Can you believe that corporal punishment was used to discipline children?
- Can you believe that teachers were fired for being pregnant and unmarried?
- Can you believe that gay staff members could not reveal their sexual identity?
- Can you believe that there were smoking areas for staff and students?
- Can you believe that long hair was forbidden on boys?
- Can you believe that girls were forbidden to wear pants to school?
- Can you believe that male teachers were required to wear coats and ties?
- Can you believe that there were boy's lines and girl's lines?
- Can you believe that the majority of sports were for boys only?
- Can you believe that there were mother/daughter and father/son banquets?

Spend some time sharing a few memories of your own that are difficult to believe today.

Your Reflection on Use of This Activity

How might you use this activity with educators/leaders from your school/district? Who would you involve/invite to participate?

Given the material presented in Chapters 1–3, how might you describe the purpose for engaging in this series of activities? Please use the space provided to record your thoughts, ideas, and questions, all of which demonstrate your concern for leading an effective professional learning experience in which you are lead learner.

_____

_____

_____

_____

_____

_____

_____

_____

Activity 3.2—Walking Forward Part 1

Purpose—To visually display the inability versus the ability of students to be able to move forward in a district due to prevailing policies, procedures, and practices in the district/site. This activity, inspired by McIntosh's (1988) work, is a powerful visual image of a percentage of students moving forward with ease and a percentage of students who never take a step forward because of current educational practices.

Readiness of Group—Beginning

Time Needed—2 hours

Materials—Written descriptions of seven diverse families. Each family description is to be inscribed on a poster for participant to hold as a reminder to the audience of which family they represent. A list of 20 practices commonly utilized within a school/district.

Process

1. Ask principals to submit a description of one family at their site.

2. Select seven families of diverse backgrounds.

3. Seven participants are selected to each represent a family.

4. Participants are each given a family description to hold and display to the audience.

5. Participants are lined up so that each participant begins at the same place.

6. Participants are told to take one step forward if the statement read is one that they believe their family can accomplish with ease.

7. Participants are told to stand still if the statement read is one that they believe their family cannot accomplish with ease.

8. Facilitator reads each statement slowly and participants proceed to either take a step forward or stand still.

9. At the end of the activity, facilitator asks the participants to reflect on their experience and elicits audience participation to discuss the blatant difference in a child's ability to move forward within a district.

Debriefing

- How did you feel as a family that did not move forward relative to the procedures of the district?
- What are reactions to these being prevalent procedures in the district?
- How did the audience feel about watching some families move very little or not at all?
- What must be our considerations?

Next Steps

In what ways does this activity support developing the 2–3 measurable goals that site administrators are to develop over the next 6–12 months? What are the corresponding goals that district administrators are to develop in support of site level efforts?

Sample Family Descriptors

Family #1

- Family of 4
- Mother and 3 children
- Caucasian
- English speaking
- Homeless and live with friends, grandmother, or in a motel
- No transportation

Family #2

- Family of 3
- Father, mother, and 1 child
- Father and mother are Latino
- Bilingual
- Mother and father are college educated
- Mother and father are both professionals

Family #3

- Family of 5
- Mother, daughter, two sons, and grandson
- Family is African American

- English speaking
- Live from paycheck to paycheck
- No savings and car was recently stolen

Family #4

- Family of 3
- Two mothers and daughter
- Mothers are Caucasian
- College educated
- Both mothers are professionals

Family #5

- Family of 2
- Mother and daughter
- Caucasian
- English speaking
- Prior drug use has resulted in loss of jobs
- Live in their minivan

Family #6

- Family of 7
- Mother, father, and 5 children
- Spanish speaking
- Parents and 3 of the children are undocumented
- Parents are illiterate

Family #7

- Family of 4
- Mother, father, and 2 children
- English speaking
- Parents are college educated professionals

Sample Statements for Having Participants Step Forward or Stay

- This family can walk into the front office of any school site or district office and be assured that someone will speak a language they understand.

- This family can afford to have their children in our music classes and athletic programs.
- The textbooks, curriculum, and instructional program regularly show families like this family.
- The library has reading books that highlight the makeup of this family.
- The parents of this family can easily attend our parent conferences held during the school day.
- This family can easily attend nighttime activities such as concerts, drama productions, and parent meetings.
- When required to fill out a lunch application and give a social security number, this family has no issue.
- When required to give an address on the emergency card, this family has no issue.
- This family can assist their children with the homework given.
- If the children go on a field trip, this family can easily give the $5 donation and send a sack lunch with their child.
- This family can afford the $5 tri-tip dinner cost at Back to School Night for the entire family.
- This family can read the information sent home in the school newsletter.
- This family is assured that all parent functions are inclusive (mother/daughter events, father/son events).
- When the teacher sends a wish list home on the first week of school, this family can easily contribute.
- When given extra credit to attend outside community events, this family can easily accommodate the cost and transportation required.
- This family has a quiet place of study, with materials readily available.
- The children of this family are likely to have health care services that ensure regular checkups and immediate health care when needed to assure excellent school attendance.
- This family can access the computer regarding school records and necessary information.
- This family can afford tutors and outside assistance if necessary.
- The children in this family are likely to be optimistic about their future as a result of their experience in our school system.

Your Reflection on Use of This Activity

How might you use this activity with educators/leaders from your school/district to build on Activity 3.1? Please use the space provided to record your thoughts, ideas, and questions, all of which demonstrate your concern for leading an effective professional learning experience in which you are lead learner.

_____

_____

_____

_____

_____

_____

_____

_____

VUSD's Implementation Journey, Year 1

Table 3.3, Template Implementation Journey: School Year 1, provides a time line of the journey in disseminating the work begun at DLT Year 1 Leadership Retreat. The school year immediately following the retreat was devoted to involving the Board of Education, credentialed

Table 3.3 Template Implementation Journey: School Year 1

Time	Activity	Participants	Outcomes
Summer leadership retreat Year 1	2-Day leadership retreat	District Leadership Team (DLT) to include psychologists, district and site administrators	Awareness and recognition of past and current practices that closed doors and did not allow students to move forward
School Year 1	Ongoing	District Leadership Team (DLT)	Aligned Guiding Principles and Mission Statement with values to implement practices that ensured open doors

educators, classified staff, parent/community members, and students in creating the district's guiding principles and mission statement.

Resource C in the back of this book provides a cumulative overview of the 3-year implementation journey begun in this chapter and continued in Chapters 4 and 5.

Going Deeper

Examining current practices in light of moribund past practices allows for perspective to be developed that may reduce defensiveness. Take a few moments alone and with colleagues to ponder information from this chapter and/or to frame your questions as you proceed to the next chapters.

Reflection

What are you learning about yourself as a leader? What more do you want to learn about your school? What more do you want to learn about the community you serve? What questions do you have as you move forward in this book? What assets do you bring to this planning process? Use the space below to record your responses.

_____

_____

_____

_____

Dialogic Professional Learning Activity

How do you, your school, and your grade level or department fit into these challenges and questions? What assets exist to support your continued work? What barriers exist to moving forward with change initiatives focused on equity and access? About what are you most enthused as we move forward? Use the space below to record the thinking of your group.

_____

_____

_____

_____

Chapter 5 moves us from the "awareness" stage of precompetence to the "doing/action" stage of *cultural competence.* With the *essential elements of cultural competence* serving as standards, you will learn the rationale for the activities and, then, immerse yourself experientially in being intentionally culturally inclusive.

In Chapter 4 we bring forward from Chapter 1 VUSD's guiding principles and mission statements developed the year following district leaders' participation in the two activities presented above. Later in the chapter we describe two activities that take the work deeper and demonstrate moving from door closers to door openers.

4

Yes, We Actually
Live Our Values

Don't tell me what you value, tell me what you do
and I'll tell you what you value.

—*Source unknown*[1]

Getting Centered

Take a moment to think of a student who is on the margins in your
school/district. The student maintains a low profile, is a "D" or "F"
student who is "passed along," and for whom your colleagues don't
have much hope for the student's academic, social, or economic future.
Please use the space below to describe as accurately as possible this
student as if you were describing her/him to a colleague or friend. In
the event you are not currently engaged with students, pick an adult
in your organization and follow the same request for description.

_____

_____

_____

_____

_____

[1] Various iterations of this epigraph have been located. The authors are aware of attributions to the quote in a letter by Malcolm X but have yet to locate a reference. If you have this or other source leads to share, we would be most appreciative.

Purpose of Chapter

The primary role of school leaders is to ensure that students have opportunity to become educated to the highest levels possible. This chapter describes how to involve school district leaders in expressing espoused inclusive values focused on narrowing and closing student access and achievement gaps among all groups of students. The two activities in this chapter involve school leaders in professional learning experiences that gauge progress in serving historically marginalized students and that illustrate valuing and using students' cultures as assets. To provide a context for the activities, we continue indicating the manner in which Dilts' Nested Levels (Dilts, 1990) and the Tools of Cultural Proficiency serve as major components for a template of change that holds students' cultures in high esteem.

From My Superintendent's Journal

As we moved forward targeting and implementing intentional practices that opened doors for all students and families, we appreciated that our work was showing results. We began to note an increase of diversity at our Back to School Nights. We invited children, provided childcare and transportation. We offered parent conferences in the evening hours which allowed our working parents to attend without losing wages. We ensured that the culminating project in a class did not require personal resources in order to compete and addressed the grading practices with an eye of equity and proficiency that resulted in an increase in student performance. We eliminated events such as "Dads and Doughnuts" and substituted with events that ensured inclusivity of all children, those with fathers in the homes as well as those without fathers in the homes. Yes, we were motivated by the small incremental success stories. We were ready to go deeper into the examination of our current practices as they related to our vision and value statement.

Some members of our organization believed that we had "arrived" and our intentional practices had opened the doors for all to walk through. Yet I found examples throughout the year illustrating that, although we were on the journey, we continued practices that required us to continue the dialogue. I displayed graphs depicting raw data such as "high school Associated Student Body (ASB) leaders by ethnicity" in contrast to "high school suspensions by ethnicity" and asked our District Leadership Team members to guess which data reflected the ASB and which reflected the suspensions, they all guessed accurately. It was true that 63% of our suspensions were Latino students, yet 20% of our Latino students represented the student ASB leaders. The results

(Continued)

were disturbing, and the fact that our guesses were 100% correct was alarming and telling. We agreed that until the results reflect the demographics of our district and until we cannot begin to guess the data, we would continue our work of equity and access.

Following a year of intentional opening door practices to ensure that every child walked forward in Ventura Unified School District (VUSD), we identified practices evident throughout the district to create a visionary school where all our best practices would be in place. We chose best practices from each of our 27 schools to create this visionary district. The children and the families of the Walking Forward I Activity remained the same, yet the system had changed dramatically. The fact was that all the components of this evolved school were components that existed in one or more of our schools due to the intentional goals.

We repeated the Walking Forward Activity 1 with the same questions, the same students and their families. There was pride and delight throughout the organization as we watched all 7 families walk forward with ease. The families and students had not changed. We had changed. I shared the various strategies that each school had incorporated over the course of the year and was most pleased to share that every one of the practices in our "visionary district" were taken from our school sites. We discussed how we could increase access as we shared best practices. We were indeed on our way to leveling the playing field and ensuring that doors were opening in VUSD to all families.

Tools of Cultural Proficiency and Nested Levels

Now, to continue developing your own approach paralleling what is being accomplished in VUSD, we turn your attention to the Table 2.1, the Conceptual Framework of Cultural Proficiency, and Table 3.1, Dilts' Nested Levels of Change. The big ideas from Chapter 2 and 3 are

- Core values, in general, serve as a guide for school districts. Inclusive core values communicate to a diverse employee workforce and community served by the school district what you intend to do. VUSD refers to their core values as Guiding Principles. The core values of Cultural Proficiency are also referred to as the *guiding principles*. If you examine the two lists of guiding principles, you will discover that the words may be different but the focus on culture as assets is consistent. Most importantly, core values are to be authentic and intended to guide actions; they are not a "paper requirement" for an external accreditation committee; although, having an authentic set of core values can provide a foundation for all the work your organization does within a self-study and an accreditation/assessment processes. The true assessment question are

- ○ *Are we who we say we are?* and
- ○ *What evidence/data do we have to demonstrate that we are who we say we are?*

• The activities in Chapter 3 lead participants to become aware of what they don't know and, therefore, what they need to learn about the diverse community they serve.

With this chapter, we continue using the Dilts' Nested Levels and the Cultural Proficiency Framework as guides for our work. Dilts' Nested Levels that address environment, behaviors, and capabilities pose these three questions that build on beliefs questions from Chapter 3:

• How will we develop new skills and/or use the skills that we have?

• In what specific behaviors will we engage?

• What do we need to begin?

With these questions in mind, you are now prepared to move along the Cultural Proficiency continuum from cultural precompetence to cultural competence. Cultural precompetence was the level where you created with your colleagues an awareness of disparities extant in your school or district. Equipped with that informed level of awareness you are prepared to take action. Cultural competence is comprised of five action oriented and interrelated standards referred to as the essential elements of cultural competence. The essential elements as standards guide us to take these actions:

• **Assess our cultural knowledge** of the diverse communities we serve; of the organizational cultural knowledge of the grade levels and departments that exist across our school district; and of our own individual cultures.
  • *VUSD illustration*—Leadership retreat during which participants engaged in Walking Forward activity that demonstrated school-based experiences based on cultural membership. As a follow-up, principals developed 2–3 measurable goals designed to reduce and preclude parents' negative experiences.
• **Value diversity** in ways that become apparent to all who visit our district, our district's website, and media reports about our district. The images on the walls and signboards of our schools,

the inclusiveness of our curriculum, the recruitment and retention of a diverse workforce all speak to a value for diversity. Diversity is expected; it is not incidental.

- *VUSD illustration*—The development of inclusive district guiding principles and mission statements, which are read at each meeting of the school board.

- **Manage the dynamics of difference** in ways that conflict is considered natural and normal. Differences of opinion and perspective occur in all personal, professional, and organizational contexts when people come together to make things happen. Cultural diversity may add complexity to such differences of opinion and is to be embraced as opportunity to learn about culturally based experiences and perspectives—and certainly not something to be avoided.

  - *VUSD illustration*—Leadership retreats during which participants experience what it feels like to be excluded and included.

- **Adapt to the diversity** of the community as it evolves and changes and as our knowledge and understanding of our community depends.

  - *VUSD illustration*—During the school year following the first leadership retreat, participants deepened their knowledge of access and achievement data and engaged teacher and staff colleagues in conversations that changed from students being identified as "underperforming" to students "being underserved."

- **Institutionalize cultural knowledge** as community knowledge and valued as being important to the professional learning of every employee.

  - *VUSD illustration*—With VUSD's guiding principles as core values, educators and staff used a "culture as assets" approach when communicating and learning with the diverse cultural groups that comprise the community served by the district.

Reflection

Pause for a moment to digest the information in this section. You may want to review Dilts' 3 questions and the *5 essential elements of cultural competence*. What questions arise for you? What thoughts are occurring to you? Are you who you say you are? What might data reveal about you and your organization? Please use this space to record your thoughts.

_____

_____

_____

_____

Inclusive Core Values

The initial summer retreat template Table 3.3, for VUSD led to an action-packed year during which school leaders reexamined and recommitted to the inclusive core values and a mission statement designed for leaders serving all students in the Ventura schools. District and school leaders took care to ensure they were not envisioning students who attended their schools a generation ago or some mythical conception of students who some might prefer to attend their schools. No, the leaders were pragmatic in valuing and embracing the cultural assets of their current students and their families.

From numerous meetings, the seven core values evolved into principles to guide the district as it moved forward. From those guiding principles, the mission statement was utilized to guide educational decisions to lead us into the next decade.

VUSD's Guiding Principles

- We will make decisions in the best interest of students.
- We will value and celebrate diversity and treat all people with dignity and respect.
- We will operate in a fiscally responsible manner.
- We will work as a team.
- We will maintain a working environment that promotes professional growth and excellence.
- We will celebrate and recognize success, creativity, and achievement through a variety of indicators.
- We will embrace families and community as partners in education.

VUSD Mission Statement

The Ventura Unified School District will educate all students in safe, healthy, and high performing schools. We will

- inspire all students to excel academically;
- honor the unique quality and diverse backgrounds of all students;

- build supportive relationships;
- guide all students to reach their full potential;
- motivate all students to successfully pursue their chosen life path; and
- engage all students to become responsible and contributing members of society.

With these statements in hand, the district leaders were ready to move forward. Not content for these statements of value and intent to be relegated to a print or digital binder where they might reside until the next accreditation visit, leaders crafted two very basic questions that guide them in virtually every decision-making opportunity:

- In what ways might this action close doors for students?
- In what ways might this action open doors for students?

Clear, straight forward, and actionable were the criteria used to developing these two questions. These two questions were to become the embodiment of the guiding principles and mission statement. They were ready to craft templates for actions based on clear and distinct core values. The next step was to engage participants in activities that would make the learning personal to each educational leader in the district.

Template Uses the Continuum to Guide Actions Based on Inclusive Values

Moving from precompetence to competence is an intentional, mindful decision that leads to action. Decisions and consequent mindful actions focused on access and equity issues are guided by VUSD's guiding principles.

You will recall that activities described in Chapter 3 were conducted in a summer retreat to foster an initial awareness of inclusion and exclusion focused on participants' experiences when they were students in preK–12 schools. It is important for this first step to be personalized for participants. Making learning personal assures attention in ways that most didactic presentations cannot achieve. The second step was to create awareness about current students' experiences of being included or excluded. As discussed above, the ensuing year was devoted to developing VUSD's guiding principles and mission statement. Their summer retreat the following year was designed to develop capacity for action. The activities that follow were selected and tailored for their community of leader learners.

It should be noted that you, your school, and your district may be able to compact the processes described thus far into a briefer amount of time than that used by VUSD. Whether spaced over a year as they did or in a more compact time frame consistent with local needs and dynamics, the most important consideration is to allow time to deeply reflect on action as well as allow for reflection-in-action. In essence, you will be reculturing your school organization. Reculturing a school or district is a process in which participants need time to uncover assumptions, deconstruct previous learning about instructional leadership, time to reflect on decisions made and to be made, and time to think deeply about what they truly value in education for the community being served.

The activities are presented in the sequence used in VUSD. Each activity is presented in lesson plan format complete with purpose statements, needed time frames, and suggested sequence of steps. Following each activity is opportunity for you to think about how the activity might be best used in your school or district context. The two activities for this chapter are

- **Walking Forward Part 2**—This activity serves to have participants experience what it is like to be moved forward when school policies and practices responds with inclusive changes.
- **I Am Activity**—This activity supports participants to experience the richness that present when we get to know our colleagues, parents, community members, and students.

Activity 4.1—Walking Forward Part 2

Purpose—To illustrate the power of system change on students' ability to move forward within a school or district. This activity serves as a follow up to Walking Forward Part 1 with a dramatic display of a student's ability to move forward when the district creates needed systemic changes.

Readiness—Intermediate

Time Needed—2 hours

Process

1. Prior to the session, ask participants to submit their examples of intentional practices/goals that have been implemented since the initial Walking Forward Part 1 activity.

2. Collect the practices and write a description of the "imaginary and ideal" school/district using the new intentional practices.

3. Bring the group back together with a reminder of what they observed in the first activity.

4. Ask the same participants to come forward and, to the extent possible, assign each participant the same family from Walking Forward Part I.

5. Give each participant the poster with the written description of the family to display during the activity.

6. Read the "imaginary and ideal" description of the school that they now attend. Clarify that they are to respond according to the new school/district description.

7. Give the same instructions to walk forward if the statement describes what they can easily do versus standing still if the statement would not be easily accomplished.

8. Read the statements slowly as the participants move forward.

Debriefing

- What happened once the system changed?
- How can we explain the fact that all students moved forward, even though the families remained the same?

- Inform the group that the imaginary/ideal school was made up of components from every school in district. Discuss ways to increase the components on campus.
- How did the participants feel in this activity versus the first activity?

Template of Sample Statements for Imaginary School

Visualize a school where . . .

- All school events, activities, and dinners are free for students who qualify for Free or Reduced lunch.
- Parent conferences are held in the afternoons and evenings to accommodate working parents and transportation is available.
- All school functions are designed to be inclusive to ensure that any family makeup is welcomed and included.
- All front offices have a staff member who is bilingual.
- School library is open until 7:00 p.m. with adult tutors to assist as needed.
- Computers are designated at the site for parent use.
- Annual wish list includes services as well as resources.
- Extracurricular activities and courses that require equipment are not charged to the families.
- Textbooks, resources, and library books are purchased with a culturally proficient lens.
- Homework and tutoring centers are provided to all students before and after school hours.
- All parents are informed that Social Security numbers are not required on Free and Reduced lunch applications.
- Parents without permanent shelter are welcome to use the school address as their place of residence.
- Transportation is provided to evening events.
- All information sent home is translated into Spanish.
- Free health clinics are provided on campus at the Family Center.
- Board policy has been changed to not allow credit to be given for individual events that require financial resources.

Your Reflection on Use of This Activity

How might you use this activity with educators/leaders from your school/district in ways that build on Activity 3.1? Please use the space provided to record your thoughts, ideas, and questions, all of which demonstrate your concern for leading an effective professional learning experience in which you are lead learner.

Activity 4.2—I Am Activity

Purpose—To share the collective diversity within the group of participants. To realize that we are rich in our collective diversity and each has a unique history. To realize that we often do not really know the identity of our colleagues, students, and families until we take the time to find out who they are.

Readiness of Group—Beginning

Time Needed—1 hour

Materials—An index card for every participant

Process

1. Distribute an index card to every participant.
2. Give instructions to write five sentences, all beginning with the words, "I am."
3. Prompt the participants to think deeply about who they are and with whom they identify.
4. Give examples such as gender, age, family, talents, sexual identity, religion, political beliefs, successes, challenges, or childhood factors.
5. Collect the cards.
6. Ask all participants to be silent and listen to the diversity in the room. Read the cards randomly without reading all 5 from any one card in succession.
7. After reading all the statements, ask participants to reflect on the diversity in the room.

Debriefing

- To what extent were identifying descriptors a surprise to you?
- To what extent did you question how much you really knew your colleagues?
- In what ways might you translate this activity to reveal how much you know about your students?

VUSD's Implementation Journey, Year 2

Table 4.1, Implementation Journey: School Template Year 2, builds on the firm foundation provided by thoughtful, districtwide consideration of VUSD's Guiding Principles and Mission Statement. The summer retreat in Year 2 deepened participants' understanding of inequity in general and with specific application to their areas of leadership responsibilities. During Year 2, school leaders—principals, assistant principals, and others involved in the summer retreat—took the experiences and information from the first two summer retreats to lead professional learning.

During this second school year two important occurrences are noteworthy. First, the district's Guiding Principles and Mission Statement are read at the open of every board meeting. Second, the districtwide mantra became, *Do we have the will and vision to open the doors that are closed?* Resource C to the back of this book compiles Table 4.1 with corresponding table from Chapters 3 and 5.

Table 4.1   Implementation Journey Template: School Year 2

Time	Activity	Participants	Outcomes
Summer leadership retreat Year 2	1 Day leadership retreat	District Leadership Team (DLT)	Identified and celebrated diversity in DLT and developed visionary school to guide development of inclusive practices
School Year 2	Ongoing	District Leadership Team (DLT)	Intentional changes of practices at district and school sites that closed/opened doors

Going Deeper

Systemic change is guided by clear, inclusive values and is intentional in design and implementation. Take a few moments alone and with colleagues to ponder information from this chapter and/or to frame your questions as you proceed to Chapter 5.

Reflection

In what ways do you describe the connection between a school/district's expressly inclusive core values and having the willingness and capacity to take actions consistent with the essential elements of cultural competence? Take a few moments and jot down the assets you bring to this task and what you need to learn in order to be effective.

_____

_____

_____

_____

Professional Learning Dialogic Activities

Where would you like for your school/district to be in three years? What are the next steps in professional learning for your school? What assets and resources are in place to support this journey? What might be some barriers to overcome along your journey? Use the space below to record your responses.

_____

_____

_____

_____

Chapter 5 describes transformative processes used in VUSD intended to meet the educational needs of an ever-changing community and student demography in the context of maintaining the school district's historical commitment to high educational standards for all students. Cultural Proficiency is described as a process of continuous professional learning in service of meeting the educational needs and aspirations of all students.

5

Continuous Learning Involves Deconstructing Our Learning

Cultural Proficiency is not a point along the continuum
to which one arrives; rather, it is the action one takes
when holding Culturally Proficient values.

—*Authors, 2015*

Getting Centered

Think of a time, personal or professional setting, where you had an "ah-ha" insightful moment that momentarily "rocked your world." Now, please don't demur and say you can't recall such an experience, you *are* a leader and effective leaders have insights to self, to others, and to situations. Take a few moments to describe the experience in details that include recollection of your feelings and reaction "in the moment." Record your recollections and insights here.

_____

_____

_____

_____

Culturally proficient leaders anticipate and name emerging problems arising from inequities and, being leaders, they direct actions intended to narrow and close access and achievement gaps. Leadership for preK–12 schools in these earliest days of the 21st century is characterized by breaking boundaries in delivering education to children and youth across racial, ethnic, gender, socioeconomic, and language demographic boundaries that were treated as unassailable barriers a generation ago. Culturally proficient leaders peer deeply into dilemmas and issues arising from inequity to extend and deepen their own learning as well as the learning of their colleagues. Culturally proficient leaders skillfully deconstruct education practices that have traditionally been accepted but have only served some students well. Educating all students to high levels relies on educational leaders' willingness and ability to foster a vision of inclusiveness that supports their educator colleagues, schools, and districts to extend their own learning in ways that continuously identifies and removes barriers to student learning. An outcome of culturally proficient leadership is embracing Cultural Proficiency as a process, not a destination at which to arrive and rest.

Purpose of This Chapter

This chapter illustrates mindsets and processes that leaders use to move themselves, their colleagues, and their schools/districts to exceed cultural competence by leading ongoing institutional learning that fosters transformative change. Cultural competence is guided by the Five Essential Elements of Cultural Competence as standards that guide *doing*. With the essential elements functioning as standards, leaders can take actions based on those standards and their progress can be indicated and measured. Cultural Proficiency is a continuous learning process that extends the inside-out process of exploring individual and institutional assumptions in ways that expects leaders to display the courage to assume that all students can learn *and* that educators can educate all learners. Cultural Proficiency is characterized by

- continuous, ongoing learning, individually and organizationally;
- commitment to socially just actions, doing what is right for students; and,
- advocacy for those who are on the margins and needing to be served differently.

On the continuum, Cultural Proficiency is where educators continue to analyze data to understand where improvements are needed and, in doing so, are willing and able to probe for assumptions embedded in educator behaviors and institutional practices. Assumptions that drive practice, when revealed, can be surfaced and examined and for the extent to which such actions might serve as door closers rather than door openers to student access and achievement. Culturally proficient leaders uncover, examine, and help change negative assumptions that allow educational leaders to be effective in providing education to diverse student populations, some of which have been historically marginalized and underserved.

From My Superintendent's Journal

At VUSD, the institutionalization of negative assumptions was manifest. The leaders of VUSD relentlessly sought to uncover the underlying inequities and the practices that were deeply rooted in the culture. Grading practices were sacred cows in VUSD and ultimately became identified as "long-standing traditions" once they came under scrutiny. When the VUSD educators were given the opportunity to ask the difficult question, "What is our confidence level that grades assigned to students are consistent, accurate, meaningful, equitable, and supportive of opening the doors for all students?" we had to pause and reflect. We discovered that our grading system did not always reflect the mission and guiding principles of our District. Grading practices such as giving extra credit to attend a community event, which required financial resources, transportation, and personal time, were commonplace. Grade point deductions were given for actions such as being tardy, not bringing supplies from home, and not participating in summer reading. Our grading practices were eliminating opportunity and consequently increasing the achievement gap for various groups of students.

Recognizing inequitable practices was not enough. The moral imperative was to take action. Board Policy was revised, conversations were started, grading committees were formed, and best practices were researched as we reaffirmed the teacher's authority. A district philosophy was established to ensure that grading and reporting practices supported the learning process and encouraged success for all students. Subcommittees created and presented modules such as "Extra Evidence Instead of Extra Credit", "Alternative to the Zero" and "Strategies for Reporting Behaviors Separately from Grades". We continue to measure the impact of this work through the evidence of student success.

The willingness and ability to probe underlying, often hidden and deeply embedded assumptions is characteristic of educators moving from the awareness created at cultural precompetence to becoming culturally competent. As educators gain insight to values, behaviors, policies, and practices that do not serve all students equitably, whether intended or unintended, they bring full attention to addressing disproportional educational outcomes.

Reflection

What is your understanding of how Cultural Proficiency is similar yet different from cultural competence? What might be some examples of culturally proficient actions? Use the space below to write your thoughts and questions.

_____

_____

_____

_____

Gaining Insight

As a school leader you know the value of insight, both yours and that of trusted colleagues. Insight is derived from vision, experience, and intuition. In preceding chapters we used the Cultural Proficiency Conceptual Framework and the Nested Levels of Organizational Change to describe the value of engaging in reflection and dialogue. Here are two important reasons that illustrate why reflection and dialogue are important communication tools that lead to insightful connections:

- To understand how assumptions are embedded in our values and behaviors
- To understand how assumptions are embedded into our schools' policies and practices (Argyris, 1993; Dilts, 1990, 1994)

Inclusive mission statements and guiding principles such as those of the Ventura Unified School District provides school leaders the opportunity to probe assumptions operating in their schools and school districts in ways that leads to understanding access and academic disparities in substantive ways. Culturally precompetent educators ask courageous questions that often reveal what we don't know, on issues and topics related to culture not part of natural discourse at the school, and what we need to learn. Too often school leaders are unaware of the racial and ethnic disparities in special education classes, who are not in advanced placement courses, and who are suspended and expelled at disproportionate rates. Equipped with these emerging awarenesses, culturally competent educators initiate actions aligned with inclusive core values that narrow and close access and achievement gaps. These actions are informed by the essential elements that serve as standards that guide educators and their actions and policies.

Culturally proficient educators advocate for continuous learning that deepens understanding of personal and institutional barriers to inclusivity. Culturally proficient leaders value, develop, and practice keen insight. This concept of self-awareness, or insight, has been central to leadership literature for generations (Hersey, 1984; Luft & Ingham, 1955). Table 5.1 is an adaptation of the Conceptual Framework from Chapter 2 designed to illustrate how and where insight leads to ever-deeper examination of underlying, hidden assumptions. Take a few moments to read and absorb information in the table.

In making sense of the table, most likely you made observations such as these:

- The behaviors described under cultural destructiveness, incapacity, and blindness are the result of negative core values held, implicitly or explicitly, about students and their cultures.
- The behaviors described under cultural precompetence, competence, and proficiency are developmental and evolve from willingness to examine assumptions and to regard students' culture as assets on which to construct their educational experience.
- Development of insight begins with cultural precompetence and is manifest in one's behaviors aligned with embracing culture as asset.
- Continuous learning, an in-depth process of constructing thought, deconstructing learning, and skill building, becomes a way of probing ever more deeply in ways that develop insight into one's own and the school's barriers that knowingly or unknowingly impede students' access to learning opportunities.

Table 5.1 Insights Guide Actions and Deeper Learning: Insights Guide Spirals of Continuous Learning

Cultural Destructiveness	Cultural Incapacity	Cultural Blindness	Cultural Precompetence	Cultural Competence	Cultural Proficiency
			Personal and Organizational Actions		
Supported by Barriers to Cultural Proficiency			**Supported by Guiding Principles of Cultural Proficiency**		
Hostility and negativity directed to cultural groups	*Dismissive and blaming people as being incapable*	*Unable or unwilling to see culture*	*Initial Awareness*	*Doing*	*Continuous Learning*
			Beginning to examine data and testimonies about inequity and disproportionality	Using essential elements to uncover blind spots and areas of ongoing learning in ways that lessens and eliminates access gaps and narrows and closes achievement gaps	Committing to continuous learning
The common denominator among these three gradients of negativity—blockage, indifference, and invisibility—is they serve to block students' access to equitable education. These actions are reflected in educators; values and behaviors and schools' policies and practices.			Probing assumptions Committing to learning		Continuing to probe assumptions Scanning environment to proactively identify inequities

Reflection

In what ways do you describe insight? How do you link insight to the continuous learning suggested by Cultural Proficiency? What questions are surfacing for you? Please use the space provided to record your thinking.

Activity 5.1—The Power of Us

Purpose—To recall past practices that either opened or closed doors for District Leadership Team (DLT) members during our personal K–12 educational experiences. To recognize the incredible power we have as educational leaders to open and close doors for others.

Readiness of Group—Intermediate

Time: 2–3 hours

Process

1. Request all DLT members to submit in writing examples of times in their K–12 experience when doors were opened and closed.

2. Select a few of the more powerful statements and ask members if they would share in front of the entire group.

3. Categorize the others in the category of Words, Rules, Consequences, Personal Resources, Culture, Expectations, and Parental Influence.

4. Share examples of submittals under each category.

5. Have members break into small groups to reflect and share additional examples.

6. End the activity with a slide depicting the power of you, me, and us.

7. Begin to prepare colleagues to examine the door closers within our system today.

Debriefing

Explore with participants what it was like to recall these experiences. After several participants have shared experiences, transition the conversation to their reactions to the categories. Finally, make the last part of the conversation to explore next steps for identifying door closers to students and families in their school and in the district.

Activity 5.2—Opening Doors for Students, Part 1

Do Our Actions Reflect Our Values?

Purpose—To critically examine practices in place within the district and determine a will and a vision to open doors that are closed. To challenge ourselves to ensure alignment of our values with our vision and mission statements and with our professional and institutional practices.

Readiness of Group—Intermediate

Time Needed—2–3 hours

Process

1. After sharing our personal experiences of doors being opened and closed by educators, we delve into our own practices.

2. Begin by reviewing the vision, mission, guiding principles of the organization with the continual question, "Do our actions reflect our values?"

3. Share the analogy of doors being wide open, cracked open, partially closed, and slammed closed.

4. Prepare staff to look at thought-provoking questions regarding current practices with a continual lens on actions versus values.

In preparation for this activity, the leader will need to identify practices that are not in alignment with the vision/mission of the district and have those categorized under the appropriate mission statement.

Debriefing

This activity is likely to challenge the core of an organization as it highlights practices that are perhaps controversial, sacred, or personal. Discuss this issue as you encourage staff to be open to the discussion. If we are not willing to challenge a practice that conflicts with our mission, then we must change the mission. We cannot have actions that do not reflect our stated values, nor can we continue practices that close doors. Now is the time to set goals to ensure that the stated practices discontinue.

Template of Sample Mission/Core Value Statements and Related Prevalent Practices

Sample of Actions That Did Not Reflect Our Stated Values:

#1—We will inspire all students to excel academically.

- Have we employed grading practices that do not accept late work?
- Have we disallowed students into GATE, Honors, or AP classes?
- Have we consistently had one bus arrive late to school?
- Have we supported referrals to special education assessment before all alternatives have been explored?
- Have we not stood up for students when there is pressure or resistance from staff?
- Have we disallowed students to go through promotion ceremonies based on behavior?
- Have we denied students the opportunity to stay at the school that has been "home" because they no longer live in the attendance area or no longer need the level of special education services?

Key Question: Do we have the will and vision to open the doors that are closed?

#2—We will honor the unique qualities and diverse backgrounds of all students.

- Have our students had to have personal funds to participate in many school activities (athletics, music, graduation, clubs, field trips)?
- Have we shown a disproportionate number of Latino males as suspensions and expulsions?
- Have we given extra credit for attending a theatrical performance on a weekend?
- Have we given assignments that require glue, glitter, cookie dough, tag boards, and so forth?
- Have we allowed others to change the names of students or staff members?

Key Question: Do we have the will and vision to open the doors that are closed?

#3—Value and celebrate diversity and treat all people with dignity and respect.

- Have we referred to difficult parents in derogatory terms and held their children accountable?
- Have we had students make Mother's Day, Father's Day, Christmas, Easter gifts?
- Have we only allowed students to go to the prom with students of the opposite sex?
- Have we denied a student lunch because they are without lunch money again?

Key Question: Do we have the will and vision to open the doors that are closed?

#4—Embrace families and communities as partners.

- Have we excluded children from Back to School Nights?
- Have we only held parent conferences and School Site Council meetings during the afternoon hours?
- Have we only conducted parent meetings in English?
- Have we held picture days, assemblies, dances on Jewish holidays?
- Have we resorted to less than polite or helpful behavior when dealing with difficult people over the phone or e-mail?
- Have we told an employee that he or she cannot take off work to attend his or her own child's event?
- Have we turned a parent away if he or she arrives 45 minutes late to their parent conference?
- Have we made assumptions about parents based on their demand, behavior, or demeanor?

Key Question: Do we have the will and vision to open the doors that are closed?

Activity 5.3—Opening Doors for Students, Part 2

Do Our Actions Reflect Our Values? To What Extent
Are We Escorting Students Through the Doors?

Purpose—To revisit the practices identified in previous Leadership Retreat and identify intentional changes that have been made to keep the doors open and aligned with the vision/mission of the district. To recognize that Cultural Proficiency requires us to do more than open the doors; it is our responsibility to escort students through the doors.

Readiness—Intermediate

Time Needed—2–3 hours

Process

1. Require all DLT members to submit the intentional changes that have occurred over the past year.
2. Array changes in PPT slides (see template that follows).
3. At the DLT meeting, spend time reviewing the slides from last year with the identified practices that did not align with the vision/mission of the district.
4. Share the new practices submitted by DLT members with the team.
5. Celebrate and honor the new practices made throughout the district.

Debriefing

Ask 3–5 members to share reactions occurring at their schools as a consequence of these new activities. Be candid in also asking about "speed bumps" and how they were handled, then probe as to the perceived benefits of having the new activities. Conclude with asking members to contrast these activities with the negative-oriented activities earlier in Activity 5.2.

Template of Emerging Practices in VUSD

- Child care provided at Back to School nights
- Preschool classes in Spanish
- English Language Advisory Committee meetings held in the neighborhood, schools
- Implementing Restorative Justice Practices
- English as Second Language (ESL) and Adult Basic and Secondary Education classes offered free of charge
- Implemented Advancement Via Individual Determination (AVID) school wide in lieu of suspensions
- Partial credits offered at the high school so student can earn more than 0 without reaching the full 5 credits
- Super Senior options for seniors who do not graduate in 4 years
- All campaign supplies are provided for student council elections (i.e., tagboard, paints, buttons)
- Staff members assigned to "students of promise" (vs. "at risk") as one-to-one mentors
- Clubs provided at recess time to assist helping students create positive interactions
- Fundraisers changed so as not to "out price" families (i.e., events that had admission costs to attend)
- Sports offered for free at lunch time (i.e., club sports have made a direct impact on students of poverty not being prepared to compete at the high school level)
- Instrumental music classes beginning at our elementary schools with the highest levels of poverty
- School libraries with computer access open evenings

Activity 5.4—Data That Demonstrate Areas of Need

Purpose—To illustrate with raw and fundamental data that we still have much work to do. To illustrate that our "guesses" were correct and until we reach a place that our "guesses" are incorrect or not obvious, we must continue our work.

Readiness—Intermediate

Time Required—1–2 hours

Process

1. Prior to the meeting, accumulate and array raw data for factors that examine ethnicity, socioeconomics, and gender. See sample graphs following this section to include data such as summer school by ethnicity, ASB by ethnicity, valedictorian by gender, suspensions by gender, pep squad by ethnicity, disrupted school activities by ethnicity, and so forth.

2. Prepare the data in graph format that is seemingly unsophisticated and readily comprehensible at a first glance. Select two areas of data and display them simultaneously without headings and ask members to guess which is the correct heading.

3. It will become clear that the guesses are accurate and easy.

4. Discuss why this is the case.

5. Substantiate that the data mandate that the work continue, but our "guess" of the results is equally indicative of the need to continue our work.

Sample Tables of Data Prepared for and Analyzed in Leadership Retreat

Activity 5.4.1:   Ethnic Profiles of Students and Teachers VUSD

	VUSD Student Enrollment Ethnic Profile	*VUSD Teacher Ethnic Profile*
Caucasian/White	45%	87%
Latino	53%	12%
African American	2%	1%

Participants were asked to make factual observations about data in Activity 5.4.1. Topics of conversation included ongoing educator recruitment efforts, cultural awareness of VUSD employees, and levels of educator interaction with cultural groups across the community.

Activity 5.4.2:   Ethnic Profiles of Summer School Participants and ASB Members

	Summer School Ethnic Profile	*Associated Student Body Ethnic Profile*
Caucasian/White	34%	74%
Latino	63%	20%
African American	3%	6%

As with the previous table, participants were asked to make factual observations about data in Activity 5.4.2. Consideration of these data led to robust conversation topics that ranged from microaggressions to systemic oppression to intentionality/mindfulness. These were not easy conversations, but they were important conversations that fostered increasing effectiveness with having challenging and necessary conversations about how to better serve the needs of all students.

Activity 5.4.3: Gender Profiles of Suspensions and Valedictorians/ Salutatorians

	Suspension Incidents Gender	*High School Valedictorian/Salutatorian Gender*
Female	20%	62%
Male	80%	38%

By the time participants received the third table about which to make factual observations, they are well schooled in how to proceed. Defensiveness begins to ebb and participants are able to engage in true dialogue—speaking and listening in ways that others can understand. Once participants began understanding one another, they moved smoothly from dialogic conversations to conversations in which they could make decisions.

Debriefing

What additional data that we could present might lead to similar observations and findings? What prior knowledge did you use to guess which slide went with which piece data? What is your reaction to seeing the data in this form? What should be the next steps?

Activity 5.5—Book Club

Purpose—To increase our individual knowledge of Cultural Proficiency, equity, and access through latest research. To discuss knowledge in small groups of colleagues with different jobs within the organization.

Readiness—Intermediate

Time Needed—30 minutes for introduction, 1 year to complete

Process

1. Select 5–10 books depending on the size of your group to allow book clubs of 8–10 people.
2. Present the books at the leadership meeting with titles, authors, and brief descriptions.
3. Have the books on display throughout the day.
4. Provide a sign-up sheet for all members to select an individual book club book.
5. Elicit one person to commit to becoming the book club leader.
6. Inform the members that the expectation is to meet 6 times during the year at venues/times of their choice.
7. Encourage members to be creative and meet at homes, restaurants, before work, after work, or during work.
8. The lead person is responsible for arranging the schedule and ensuring that all members are included and involved.
9. Be prepared to share your knowledge as a club with the entire DLT at the end of the year.
10. District leader is responsible for purchasing the books and distributing to all members.

Debriefing

At the end of the year, host a one-hour meeting to discuss experiences with the Book Club. Conversation should focus more on the experience of the Book Club rather than be erstwhile "book reports." Focus conversation on reflections during reading books and insights gained from dialogic conversations about books.

Sample Book Club

- *Culturally Proficient Collaboration: Use and Misuse of School Counselors*—Diana L. Stephens & Randall B. Lindsey, (2011). Thousand Oaks, CA: Corwin
- *Culturally Proficient Education: An Asset-Based Response to Conditions of Poverty*—Randall B. Lindsey, Michelle S. Karns, & Keith Myatt, (2010). Thousand Oaks, CA: Corwin.
- *Culturally Proficient Leadership: The Personal Journey Begins Within*—Raymond D. Terrell & Randall B. Lindsey
- *Culturally Proficient Learning Communities: Confronting Inequities Through Collaborative Curiosity*—Delores B. Lindsey, Linda D. Jungwirth, Jarvis V.N.C. Pahl, & Randall B. Lindsey. (2009). Thousand Oaks, CA: Corwin.
- *Courageous Conversations About Race*—Glenn Singleton & Curtis Linton. (2006). Thousand Oaks, CA: Corwin.
- *Involving Latino Families in Schools: Raising Student Achievement Through Home-School Partnerships*—Concha Delgado Gaitan. (2004). Thousand Oaks, CA: Corwin.
- *Teaching Boys Who Struggle in School: Strategies That Turn Underachievers Into Successful Learners*—Kathleen Palmer Cleveland. (2011). ASCD.
- *The Equity Framework*—Curtis Linton. (2011). Thousand Oaks, CA: Corwin.
- *The Principal as Leader of the Equitable School*—Ontario Principals' Council. (2012). Thousand Oaks, CA: Corwin.

VUSD's Implementation Journey, Year 3

Table 5.2, Template Implementation Journey: School Year 3, extended and deepened the work that had been underway for the previous two years. By the end of this third year all VUSD employees were apprised and involved with issues related to narrowing and closing access and achievement gaps.

Resource C in the back of this book serves to compile Tables 3.3, 4.1, and 5.1 to provide an overview of the major activities for VUSD's implementation journey.

Table 5.2   Template Implementation Timeline: School Year 3

Time	Activity	Participants	Outcomes
Summer leadership retreat Year 3	1-Day District Leadership Team (DLT)	District Leadership Team (DLT)	Refined opening door practices and celebrated intentional practices with utilization of data as focus
School Year 3	Ongoing	District Leadership Team (DLT)	Increased intentional practices to open doors for all students/families

Going Deeper

At the beginning of this chapter we indicated that Cultural Proficiency is characterized by at least three indicators:

- Continuous, ongoing learning, individually and organizationally
- Commitment to socially just actions, doing what is right for students
- Advocacy for those who are on the margins and need to be served differently

Take a few moments individually and later with colleagues to think deeply about information in this chapter and/or to frame your intentions as you proceed to the Epilogue.

Reflection

Thinking about the three indicators of Cultural Proficiency, what thoughts, considerations, or questions are occurring to you? Then, list the assets you bring to the work of Cultural Proficiency? What might be some assets that Cultural Proficiency can bring to the work that needs to be done in your context and the commitments you are willing to make for the work to be effective.

_____

_____

_____

_____

Professional Learning Dialogic Activities

Building on the dialogic question from Chapter 4, where would you like for your school/district to be in three years, what structures are in place in your school/district to facilitate becoming culturally proficient? What are the next steps in professional learning for your school? What assets and resources are in place to support this journey?

_____

_____

_____

_____

_____

_____

The Epilogue reviews data to indicate progress being made by the Ventura Unified School District and brings together the "look fors" introduced in the Prologue. Last, you are provided opportunity to plan your next steps.

Epilogue

This book combined a superintendent's narrative with a template that has led school leaders at all levels to experience and exercise leadership that is addressing historical inequities related to student access and achievement. We opened with a prologue that unites a district's story with a template for designing and initiating a process of change within a school district. We close by sharing progress being made in that district.

The Ventura Unified School District (VUSD) has used state and federal reform initiatives and accompanying resources to address access and academic achievement disparities among demographic/cultural groups of their students. The district engaged in a two-tiered self-examination process to uncover assumptions held by the district as an organization and by educators themselves. The intent of the self-assessment has been to redesign approaches to educating all children and youth to high levels. The district revisioned organizational policies and practices as well as educator values and behaviors in ways that embrace healthy assumptions and beliefs about students. The emergent policies and practices of the district and the values and beliefs of educators are grounded in the belief that VUSD students are capable of high academic achievement and that VUSD educators are capable of teaching and leading students to academic and social success.

Data Indicating Progress Being Made in VUSD

Findings presented in this section indicate a correlative, not causal, relationship among the initiatives described in this book and the data collected. VUSD has a long tradition of state-of-the-art approaches to curriculum, instruction, professional development/learning, assessment, and parent/community engagement. We began this book by acknowledging the unintended consequences of past practices and to bring to full view disparate and disproportional outcomes.

By bringing inequities into full light, the district crafted inclusive guiding principles, vision, and mission statements. Any magic these guiding documents possess now is due solely to the deep and courageous conversations among leaders of the VUSD. These conversations led to recommitting to educating all students in inclusive ways that embraces their cultures as assets, not deficits. The data presented here are intended to illustrate through slope and trajectory that VUSD efforts are on the ascent and serving students in multiple ways, not just a focus on outcomes such as mathematics and language arts test scores.

Most important, the work of addressing inequities is not rocket science! Using the lens of Cultural Proficiency to authentically address inequities is about heart. Being willing to examine personal and organizational assumptions is consistent with the admonition of the golden rule to do to others as you would have them do to you. The trends are undeniable. Take a few moments and notice the trends in suspension, expulsion, dropout, language redesignation, language proficiency, language arts, and mathematics data.

Table E.1 clearly indicates a decline in suspensions across the district from 2008 to 2014. Note that the rate of suspensions has declined by more than 50%.

Table E.1:   Suspension Summary 2008–2014

2008–2009	2009–2010	2010–2011	2011–2012	2012–2013	2013–2014
12%	10%	8%	8%	6%	5%

As you think about the data in Table E.1, what questions and observations occur to you?

Table E.2 continues with student discipline issues by showing the downward trend of expulsions from 2008 to 2014. Note the precipitous drop by over two-thirds in this 6-year period.

Table E.2:   Expulsion Summary 2008–2014

2008–2009	2009–2010	2010–2011	2011–2012	2012–2013	2013–2014
61	37	47	48	37	17

What questions occur to you as you look at the downward trend in expulsions?

Table E.3 shows a 40% decrease in dropout rates over a recent 5-year period.

Table E.3: Dropout Rates 2008–2012

2008–2009	*2011–2012*	*2012–2013*
10.70%	10.40%	6.10%

Thinking about this downward trend in dropout rates, what questions and observations occur to you?

Table E.4 shows an increased rate of more than 800% in students being redesignated as English fluent over the most recent 10-year period.

Table E.4: Language Census Student Redesignation Rates 2003–2013

2003	*2005*	*2009*	*2013*
33	159	256	283

What questions and observations occur to you in thinking about the marked upward trend in students being redesignated?

Table E.5 indicates an over 50% increase in English proficiency as measured by the California English Language Development Test over the most recent 10-year period.

Table E.5: Proficiency in English, California English Language Development Test (CELDT)

2003–2004	*2009–2010*	*2012–2013*
34.5%	51.6%	56.2%

As you think about the data in Table E.5, what questions and observations occur to you?

Table E.6 depicts increased achievement in English Language Arts over the most recent 10-year period as measured by a California assessment exam, Standardized Testing and Reporting (STAR). Students in Grade 3 test scores across the district are trending upward steadily, and students in Grades 7 and 11 are trending up at an even faster rate.

Table E.6:   STAR Results English Language Arts 2002–2003, 2006–2007, and 2011–2012

Year	Grade 3	Grade 7	Grade 11
2002–2003	40	48	39
—	—	—	—
2006–2007	43	57	53
2011–2012	47	67	62

As you think about the English Language Arts trend data for the identified grade levels in Table E.6, what questions and observations do you have?

Table E.7 reports for the same time period and grade levels that were reported for English Language Arts also using the mandated California assessment. With mathematics, the trend for 7th grade is for substantial gains while 3rd and 11th grade increases slope upward.

Table E.7:   STAR Results Mathematics 2002–2003, 2006–2007, and 2011–2012

Year	Grade 3	Grade 7	Grade 11
2002–2003	54	37	42
2006–2007	68	54	47
2011–2012	64	56	49

In reading the Mathematics trends in Table E.7, what observations and questions do you have?

Reflection

Thinking about these data, what thoughts and questions are arising for you as you think about your school or district? What might be some trends in your school/district? How might you locate similar data? What additional data do you want to gather? The space below is to record your responses.

_____

_____

_____

_____

The Look Fors—Charting Your Learning

In the Prologue, we invited you to be mindful of four interdependent, yet interrelated components to be treated as "look fors" as you read the text. The four "look fors" were intended to support your professional learning and successful use in your school/district. In this final section of the book you are provided the opportunity to summarize briefly your learning and to indicate next steps using the "look fors":

- **Tools of Cultural Proficiency**—Descriptions of the four tools that either taught, refreshed, or deepened your understanding and facility with the tools in your professional context.
  - I learned or affirmed:

  - Next steps for me and/or my school/district:

- **Activities**—A progression of professional learning opportunities that have been field-tested for professionals in your school/district.
  - The activities can be used by me or my district in these ways:

  - To use the activities with fidelity, I and my school/district will need to:

- **Reflection**—Opportunities for your and others' individual learning in terms of personal and professional core values and behaviors/actions that open and escort students through doors in ways that ensure equitable access and achievement in all phases of the school experience.

o To assess the inclusiveness of my and my school/district's authentic vision, mission, and core values I must:

o Next steps to ensure my and my school/district's developing an inclusive vision, mission, and core values are:

- **Dialogue**—Opportunities for school and district professional learning that analyzes and alters, as necessary, policies and prevalent practices that provide educators with the means for opening and escorting students to equitable opportunities and achievement outcomes throughout their school experiences.
  o Next steps to engage me and my school/district in professional learning that analyzes and alters, as necessary, policies and practices that open doors and escort students through to equitable opportunities begin with these three steps:

     Step 1—

     Step 2—

     Step 3—

Final Words

The purpose of this book was to illustrate that students can learn and that educators can educate. This was a story of resourceful, responsible, and moral leadership. This is a book about commitment and continuous learning. This is a book about opening doors and escorting students.

As the superintendent makes her transition from the district after 35 years of service to teaching in the Graduate School of Education at California Lutheran University, she is proud to know that leadership with a culturally proficient lens will remain the foundational value and belief system throughout the district.

The staff of Ventura Unified are primed to continue and strengthen the work of the past. Their commitment and understanding of Cultural Proficiency will ensure that all students move forward as they are escorted through open doors.

Resource A
Book Study Guide

Prologue
Chapter 1—What Frames Us, Defines Us

Content Questions to Consider

- How would you describe "framing" to someone who hasn't read this chapter?
- In the context of this book, how do you describe "safe space"?
- Briefly describe "door closers" and "door openers."
- Personal Reaction Questions to Consider
  - What is your reaction to the intent of this book?
  - What is your reaction to examining and discussing equity, access, and achievement gaps in your school?

Chapter 2—Culturally Proficient Leadership Fosters Transformative Change

Content Questions to Consider

- Name the Tools of Cultural Proficiency.
- In what ways do you differentiate among transactional, transformational, and transformative leadership?
- In what ways do you describe the *Inside-Out Process*?
- How do reflection and dialogue support the *Inside-Out Process*?
- In what ways might you describe the importance of Sinek's *what, how,* and *why* questions?
- Describe how and why culture is embraced as an asset to support Cultural Proficiency.
- In what ways are the Guiding Principles as core values consistent with how you view yourself and your school?

- Explain how the Guiding Principles serve to counter the Barriers to Cultural Proficiency.
- In what ways will the Essential Elements provide you with "action" steps on your journey toward Cultural Proficiency?

Personal Reaction Questions to Consider

- How might you either begin or deepen a consideration of equitable practices in your school or district?
- What is your reaction to the Barriers section? To the Guiding Principles as core values?
  - Describe the manner in which the Essential Elements are informed and supported by the Guiding Principles.
  - In what ways do the Essential Elements serve as standards for personal, professional behavior?
- What is your reaction, personally or professionally, as you become acquainted with the Tools?
- What more do you want to know/learn about Cultural Proficiency?

Chapter 3—Change Begins With Core Value and Belief Statements

Content Questions to Consider

- In what ways do you differentiate "espoused' from "lived" values?
- How might you describe the importance of Dilts' Nested Levels?
- How might you describe cultural competence as creating an initial awareness? What are some examples?

Personal Reaction Questions to Consider

- What is your reaction to "espoused" versus "lived" values? How would you describe the authenticity of your school/district's espoused values?
- To what extent would you be comfortable leading Activities 3.1 and 3.2?
- What are your next steps with your school/district?

Chapter 4—Yes, We Actually Live Our Values

Content Questions to Consider

- In what active ways do the Nested Levels inform and support cultural competence?
- What are illustrations educator and schools' culturally competent behaviors, policies, and practices?

Personal Reaction Questions to Consider

- What is your reaction to this chapter?
- To what extent does the intentionality of cultural competence resonate with you?

Chapter 5—Continuous Learning Involves Deconstructing Our Learning

Content Questions to Consider

- In what ways does Cultural Proficiency evolve from cultural competence?
- What are illustration educator and schools' culturally proficient behaviors, policies, and practices?

Personal Reaction Questions to Consider

- What is your reaction to this chapter?
- In what ways do you want to develop as leader?
- In what ways is a value for social justice evident in your leadership style and behaviors?

Resource B

Cultural Proficiency Books' Essential Questions

Book	Authors	Focus and Essential Questions
Cultural Proficiency: A Manual for School Leaders, 3rd ed., 2009	Randall B. Lindsey, Kikanza Nuri Robins, & Raymond D. Terrell	This book is an introduction to Cultural Proficiency. The book provides readers with extended discussion of each of the tools and the historical framework for diversity work. • What is Cultural Proficiency? How does Cultural Proficiency differ from other responses to diversity? • In what ways do I incorporate the Tools of Cultural Proficiency into my practice? • How do I use the resources and activities to support professional development? • How do I identify barriers to student learning? • How do the Guiding Principles and Essential Elements support better education for students? • What does the "inside-out" process mean for me as an educator? • How do I foster challenging conversations with colleagues? • How do I extend my own learning?

| *Culturally Proficient Instruction: A Guide for People Who Teach, 3rd ed., 2012* | Kikanza Nuri-Robins, Randall B. Lindsey, Delores B. Lindsey, & Raymond D. Terrell | This book focuses on the five essential elements and can be helpful to anyone in an instructional role. This book can be used as a workbook for a study group.

• What does it mean to be a culturally proficient instructor?
• How do I incorporate Cultural Proficiency into a school's learning community processes?
• How do we move from "mind set" or "mental model" to a set of practices in our school?
• How does my "cultural story" support being effective as an educator with my students?
• In what ways might we apply the Maple View Story to our learning community?
• In what ways can I integrate the guiding principles of Cultural Proficiency with my own values about learning and learners?
• In what ways do the Essential Elements as standards inform and support our work with the Common Core standards?
• How do I foster challenging conversations with colleagues?
• How do I extend my own learning? |
| *The Culturally Proficient School: An Implementation Guide for School Leaders, 2005 (2nd ed., 2013).* | Randall B. Lindsey, Laraine M. Roberts, & Franklin Campbell Jones | This book guides the reader to examine her or his school as a cultural organization and to design and implement approaches to dialogue and inquiry.

• In what ways do "Cultural Proficiency" and "school leadership" help me close achievement gaps?
• What are the communication skills I need master to support my colleagues when focusing on achievement gap topics?
• How do "transactional" and "transformational" changes differ and inform closing achievement gaps in my school/district? |

		• How do I foster challenging conversations with colleagues? • How do I extend my own learning?
Culturally Proficient Coaching: Supporting Educators to Create Equitable Schools, 2007	Delores B. Lindsey, Richard S. Martinez, & Randall B. Lindsey	This book aligns the essential elements with Costa and Garmston's Cognitive Coaching model. The book provides coaches, teachers, and administrators a personal guidebook with protocols and maps for conducting conversations that shift thinking in support of all students achieving at levels higher than ever before. • What are the coaching skills I need in working with diverse student populations? • In what ways do the Tools of Cultural Proficiency and Cognitive Coaching's States of Mind support my addressing achievement issues in my school? • How do I foster challenging conversations with colleagues? • How do I extend my own learning?
Culturally Proficient Inquiry: A Lens for Identifying and Examining Educational Gaps, 2008	Randall B. Lindsey, Stephanie M. Graham, R. Chris Westphal Jr., & Cynthia L. Jew	This book uses protocols for gathering and analyzing student achievement and access data. Rubrics for gathering and analyzing data about educator practices are also presented. A CD accompanies the book for easy downloading and use of the data protocols. • How do we move from the "will" to educate all children to actually developing our "skills" and doing so? • In what ways do we use the various forms of student achievement data to inform educator practice? • In what ways do we use access data (e.g., suspensions, absences, enrollment in special education or gifted classes) to inform schoolwide practices? • How do we use the four rubrics to inform educator professional development? • How do I foster challenging conversations with colleagues? • How do I extend my own learning?

Culturally Proficient Leadership: The Personal Journey Begins Within, 2009	Raymond D. Terrell, & Randall B. Lindsey	This book guides the reader through the development of a cultural autobiography as a means to becoming an increasingly effective leader in our diverse society. The book is an effective tool for use by leadership teams. • How did I develop my attitudes about others' cultures? • When I engage in intentional cross-cultural communication, how can I use those experiences to heighten my effectiveness? • In what ways can I grow into being a culturally proficient leader? • How do I foster challenging conversations with colleagues? • How do I extend my own learning?
Culturally Proficient Learning Communities: Confronting Inequity Through Collaborative Curiosity, 2009	Delores B. Lindsey, Linda D. Jungwirth, Jarvis V.N.C. Pahl, & Randall B. Lindsey	This book provides readers a lens through which to examine the purpose, the intentions, and the progress of learning communities to which they belong, or wish to develop. School and district leaders are provided protocols, activities, and rubrics to engage in actions focused on the intersection of race, ethnicity, gender, social-class, sexual orientation and identity, faith, and ableness with the disparities in student achievement. What is necessary for a learning community to become a "culturally proficient learning community"? • What is organizational culture and how do I describe my school's culture in support of equity and access? • What are "curiosity" and "collaborative curiosity" and how do I foster them at my school/district? • How will "breakthrough questions" enhance my work as a learning community member and leader?

		• How do I foster challenging conversations with colleagues? • How do I extend my own learning?
The Cultural Proficiency Journey: Moving Beyond Ethical Barriers Toward Profound School Change, 2010	Franklin Campbell Jones, Brenda Campbell Jones, & Randall B. Lindsey	This book explores Cultural Proficiency as an ethical construct. It makes transparent the connection between values, assumptions, and beliefs and observable behavior making change possible and sustainable. The book is appropriate for book study teams. • In what ways does "moral consciousness" inform and support my role as an educator? • How does a school's "core values" become reflected in assumptions held about students? • What steps do I take to ensure that my school and I understand any low expectations we might have? • How do we recognize that our low expectations serve as ethical barriers? • How do I foster challenging conversations with colleagues? • How do I extend my own learning?
Culturally Proficient Education: An Assets-Based Response to Conditions of Poverty, 2010	Randall B. Lindsey, Michelle S. Karns, & Keith Myatt	This book is written for educators to learn how to identify and develop the strengths of students from low-income backgrounds. It is an effective learning community resource to promote reflection and dialogue. • What are "assets" that students bring to school? • How do we operate from an "assets-based" perspective? • What are my and my school's expectations about students from low income and impoverished backgrounds? • How do I foster challenging conversations with colleagues? • How do I extend my own learning?

Culturally Proficient Collaboration: Use and Misuse of School Counselors, 2011	Diana L. Stephens, & Randall B. Lindsey	This book uses the lens of Cultural Proficiency to frame the American Association of School Counselor's performance standards and Education Trust's Transforming School Counseling Initiative as means for addressing issues of access and equity in schools in collaborative school leadership teams. • How do counselors fit into achievement-related conversations with administrators and teachers? • What is the "new role" for counselors? • How does this "new role" differ from existing views of school counselor? • What is the role of site administrators in this new role of school counselor? • How do I foster challenging conversations with colleagues? • How do I extend my own learning?
A Culturally Proficient Society Begins in School: Leadership for Equity, 2011	Carmella S. Franco, Maria G. Ott, & Darline P. Robles	This book frames the life stories of three superintendents through the lens of Cultural Proficiency. The reader is provided the opportunity to design or modify his or her own leadership for equity plan. • In what ways is the role of school superintendent related to equity issues? • Why is this topic important to me as a superintendent or aspiring superintendent? • What are the leadership characteristics of a culturally proficient school superintendent? • How do I foster challenging conversations with colleagues? • How do I extend my own learning?
The Best of Corwin: Equity, 2012	Randall B. Lindsey, Ed.	This edited book provides a range of perspectives of published chapters from prominent authors on topics of equity, access, and diversity. It is designed for use by school study groups.

		• In what ways do these readings support our professional learning? • How might I use these readings to engage others in learning conversations to support all students learning and all educators educating all students?
Culturally Proficient Practice: Supporting Educators of English Learning Students, 2012	Reyes L. Quezada, Delores B. Lindsey, & Randall B. Lindsey	This book guides readers to apply the 5 Essential Elements of Cultural Competence to their individual practice and their school's approaches to equity. The book works well for school study groups. • In what ways do I foster support for the education of English learning students? • How can I use action research strategies to inform my practice with English learning students? • In what ways might this book support all educators in our district/school? • How do I foster challenging conversations with colleagues? • How do I extend my own learning?
A Culturally Proficient Response to LGBT Communities: A Guide for Educators, 2013	Randall B. Lindsey, Richard Diaz, Kikanza Nuri-Robins, Raymond D. Terrell, & Delores B. Lindsey	This book guides the reader to understand sexual orientation in a way that provides for the educational needs of all students. The reader explores values, behaviors, policies and practices that impact Lesbian, Gay, Bisexual, and Transgender students, educators, and parents/guardians. • How do I foster support for LGBT colleagues, students, and parents/guardians? • In what ways does our school represent a value for LGBT members? • How can I create a safe environment for all students to learn? • To what extent is my school an environment where it is safe for the adults to be open about their sexual orientation? • How do I reconcile my attitudes toward religion and sexuality with my responsibilities as a PreK–12 educator?

		• How do I foster challenging conversations with colleagues? • How do I extend my own learning?
Culturally Proficient Learning Communities	Delores B. Lindsey, Karen M. Kearney, Delia Estrada, Raymond D. Terrell, & Randall B. Lindsey	This book guides the reader to view and use the Common Core State Standards (CCSS) as a vehicle for ensuring all demographic groups of students are fully prepared for college and careers. • In what ways do I use this book to deepen my learning about equity? • In what ways do I use this book to deepen my learning about CCSS? • In what ways do I use this book with colleagues to deepen our work on equity and on the CCSS? • How can I and we use the Action Planning guide as an overlay for our current school planning?
Opening Doors: An Implementation Template for Cultural Proficiency, 2016	Trudy T. Arriaga & Randall B. Lindsey	This book serves as a template for school leaders to use in determining levels of inclusiveness in their schools/districts. • In what ways do I use this book to deepen my understanding of equity and inclusiveness in action? • In what ways do I lead to become aware of underlying core values that limit access to students and families? • In what ways do I lead my school/district to develop and live authentic and inclusive core values and mission statements? • How do I extend my own learning?

Resource C
Ventura Unified School District Template Implementation Journey

School Years 1–3

	Time	Activity	Participants	Outcomes
Chapter 3	Summer leadership retreat Year 1	2-Day leadership retreat	District Leadership Team (DLT) to include psychologists, district and site administrators	Awareness and recognition of past and current practices that closed doors and did not allow students to move forward
	School Year 1	Ongoing	District Leadership Team (DLT)	Aligned Guiding Principles and Mission Statement with our values to implement practices that ensured open doors

Chapter 4	Summer leadership retreat Year 2	1 Day leadership retreat	District Leadership Team (DLT)	Identified and celebrated diversity in DLT and developed visionary school to guide development of inclusive practices
	School Year 2	Ongoing	District Leadership Team (DLT)	Intentional changes of practices at district and school sites that closed/opened doors
Chapter 5	Summer leadership retreat Year 3	1 Day District Leadership Team (DLT)	District Leadership Team (DLT)	Refined opening door practices and celebrated intentional practices with utilization of data as continued focus
	School Year 3	Ongoing	District Leadership Team (DLT)	Increased intentional practices to open doors for all students/families

Resource D

Cultural Proficiency Implementation Model for Large-Scale, Long-Term Change

Focused on Equity for All Students

Delores B. Lindsey, Raymond D. Terrell, and
Randall B. Lindsey

April 29, 2015

*T*he *Tools of Cultural Proficiency* enable educational leaders to respond effectively in cross-cultural environments by using a powerful set of interrelated tools to guide personal and organizational change (Cross, Bazron, Dennis, & Isaacs, 1989; Lindsey, Nuri Robins, & Terrell, 2009). Through identifying personal and institutional barriers for students' access and equity and committing to lived core values for inclusion, culturally proficient leaders take actions that invite in all students and ensure their academic success. The tools for culturally proficient practices allow school leaders to focus on students and their cultural communities as assets in ways that overcome barriers to student success. When Cultural Proficiency is introduced and embraced in a school or throughout the district as a change initiative, educators have an opportunity to select from pathways for fully implementing an action plan.

Change can begin anywhere in a school district; but to have systemic change that stands the test of time, the higher in the hierarchy of the school district that change is embraced as natural and normal, the more likely the change initiative will be embraced throughout the organization (Dilts, 1990, 1994; Fullan, 2011). Bateson and Dilts' *Nested*

Levels of Learning, as adapted by Garmston and Wellman (1999), serves as a model of behavioral and organizational change. Figure D.1 displays this nested level model, incorporated with Hargreaves and Fullan's (2012) descriptions of professional growth, for implementing and directing change efforts, is predicated on the notion that behavioral and observable changes most significantly occur when all levels of the school/district are involved. Irrespective of where the change initiative is introduced, the initiative most directly impacts behaviors of colleagues at that level and below that level in the school/district. Therefore, when the change initiative is embraced at the leadership level of the school district priorities are unambiguous; everyone is involved. Change initiatives are intentional, supported, and involve the totality of the district.

Figure D.2 demonstrates the commitment and collaboration of partners informed by the Tools of Cultural Proficiency. And Figure D.3 shows the various pathways for leverage points that change initiatives can enter using the systems approach (Senge et al., 2000). This figure offers three options; however, change leaders may initiate Cultural Proficiency at any point in the organization or as an individual initiative for personal change. Based on an assessment of cultural knowledge and student needs, leaders will determine the best pathway for change. Lists of books to support individual and organization professional learning are provided for each pathway

- Tables D.1–D.3 provide the implementation Outcomes, Strategies, Content and Process, and Sustainability Plan for Large-Scale Change.

Figure D.1 Creating and Sustaining Organizational Change Through the Lens of Cultural Proficiency

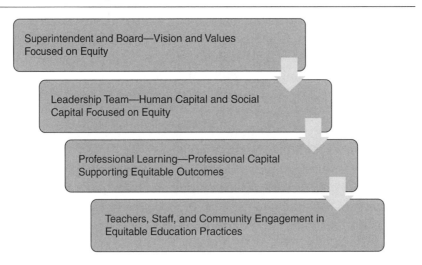

Figure D.2   The Tools of Cultural Proficiency

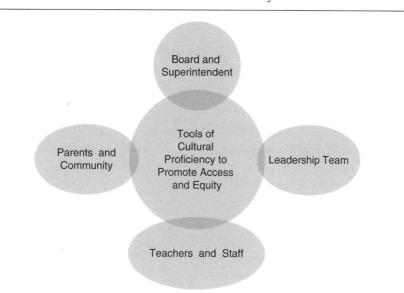

Figure D.3   Pathways for Implementation

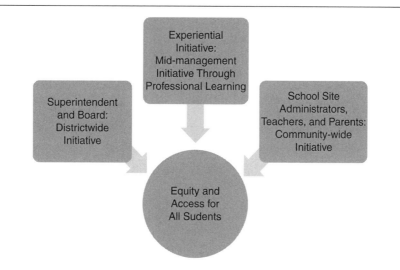

Book Study Titles Associated With Roles and Implementation Pathways

Superintendent

- *Culturally Proficient Leadership*—Terrell & Lindsey
- *Cultural Proficiency: A Manual for School Leaders*, 3rd ed.—Lindsey, Nuri Robins, & Terrell

- *Culturally Proficient Schools*, 2nd ed.—Lindsey, Roberts, & Campbell Jones
- *Culturally Proficient Society*—Franco, Ott, & Roble
- *Opening Doors*—Arriaga & Lindsey

Leadership Team

- Culturally Proficient Leadership—Terrell & Lindsey
- Cultural Proficiency: A Manual for School Leaders, 3rd ed.—Lindsey, Nuri Robins, & Terrell
- *Culturally Proficient Schools*, 2nd ed.—Lindsey, Roberts, & Campbell Jones
- *The Cultural Proficiency Journey*—Campbell Jones, Campbell Jones, & Lindsey
- *Opening Doors*—Arriaga & Lindsey

Administrators

- *Culturally Proficient Leadership*—Terrell & Lindsey
- *Cultural Proficiency: A Manual for School Leaders*, 3rd ed.—Lindsey, Nuri Robins, & Terrell
- *Culturally Proficient Schools*, 2nd Ed.—Lindsey, Roberts, & Campbell Jones
- *Culturally Proficient Coaching*—Lindsey, Martinez, & Lindsey
- *Opening Doors*—Arriaga & Lindsey

Teachers and Staff

- *Culturally Proficient Instruction*, 3rd Ed.—Nuri Robins, Lindsey, Lindsey, & Terrell
- *Culturally Proficient Learning Communities*—Lindsey, Jungwirth, Pahl, & Lindsey
- *Culturally Proficient Schools*, 2nd ed.—Lindsey, Roberts, & Campbell Jones
- *Culturally Proficient Inquiry*—Lindsey, Graham, Westphal Jr., & Jew
- *Culturally Proficient Coaching*—Lindsey, Martinez, & Lindsey
- *Culturally Proficient Education* (Poverty)—Lindsey, Karns, & Myatt

- *Culturally Proficient Practice* (Student learning English as additional language)—Quezada, Lindsey, & Lindsey
- *Culturally Proficient Collaboration* (Counseling)—Stephens & Lindsey
- *A Culturally Proficient Response to the Common Core*—Lindsey, Kearney, Estrada, Terrell, & Lindsey

Parents and Community Members

- *Culturally Proficient Schools*, 2nd ed.—Lindsey, Roberts, & Campbell Jones
- *The Cultural Proficiency Journey*—Campbell Jones, Campbell Jones, & Lindsey

Table D.1   Outcomes and Strategies

Time	*Activity*
• Narrowing and closing access and education gaps • Reducing and eliminating disproportional outcomes regarding student discipline/behavior and academic placement	• Site-based inquiry that involves data collection and analyses through lens of Cultural Proficiency • Examining for inclusive and equitable instructional program • Examining for inclusive and equitable curricular and cocurricular programs • Being intentional about inclusive parent and community engagement • Developing formative and summative assessment strategies that inform continuous improvement framework (growth mindset)

Table D.2   Key Content and Process Components

Content	*Processes*
• Understand relationship between cultural values, beliefs, and assumptions with/to behaviors. • Increase understanding of cultural assumptions and their influence on behavior. • Deepen understanding that leads to actions as leverage points for personal and organizational change.	• Learn four foundational tools in context using exercises and activities. • Engage in use of book study guides for personal reflection and dialog with colleagues. • Collect and analyze school/district data. • Analyze espoused values, beliefs with collected data to compare to theory-in-action. • Surface assumptions through reflection and dialog. • Examine all district/schoolwide programs and resources that support teaching and learning (e.g., District Safety Plan, District hiring practices, Parent Involvement Plans, Parent-Teacher agreements, School Discipline Plans, Assessment, Curriculum, Instruction Plans, Special Education Inclusive Plans, Meeting English Learner Needs Plans, Who takes What courses? Master Schedule.). Analyze disproportionality data. • Plan actions to meet needs and close gaps. (Develop a Culturally Proficient Action Plan.)

Table D.3 Sustainability for Long-Term, Large-Scale Change

Growing our own Culturally Proficient Leaders	Year One	Year Two	Year Three
Cohort One: Level One 30–40 member cadre of district-wide educators: district office and site administrators, teachers, staff members, and parents.	**Focus of training:** *What is Cultural Proficiency and why do we need it?* Understand the 4 Tools of Cultural Proficiency and the response to educational and equity gaps.	**Focus of training:** *How do we apply the Tools?* Collect site-based data and analyze how Cultural Proficiency can inform practice. Use 5 Essential Elements to turn values into action.	**Focus of training:** *How do we assess that what we are doing is working?* Develop case studies from action research models (Year 2) to demonstrate growth over time for all demographic groups using multiple data sources.
	(3–4 Days) Book Study: *Manual for School Leaders*	Book Study: *Culturally Proficient Learning Communities,* or *Inquiry* (2 days f2f)	Book Study: *Schools* (2 days f2f)
Cohort One, Level Two: A smaller cadre of educators from Level One participants		**Focus of training:** Use trainer-of-trainer model to prepare participants to teach the 4 Tools of Cultural Proficiency	
		(3 days) Book Study: *Culturally Proficient Leaders*	

(Continued)

Table D.3 (Continued)

Cohort One, Level Three: **A smaller cadre of educators from Level Two participants**		**Focus of training:** Complete trainer-of-trainers model to include facilitation and coaching skills. (4 days) Book Study: *Culturally Proficient Coaching*	**Focus of training:** *How do we assess that what we are doing is working?* Develop case studies from action research models (Year 2) to demonstrate growth over time for all demographic groups using multiple data sources. Book Study: *Schools* (2 days f2f)
Cohort Two, Level One: **(Begins in Year Two)** 30–40 member cadre of district-wide educators: district office and site administrators, teachers, staff members, and parents.	**Focus of training:** *What is Cultural Proficiency and why do we need it?* Understand the 4 Tools of Cultural Proficiency and the response to educational and equity gaps. (3-4 Days) Book Study: *Manual for School Leaders*	**Focus of training:** *How do we apply the Tools?* Collect site-based data and analyze how Cultural Proficiency can inform practice. Use 5 Essential Elements to turn values into action. Book Study: *Culturally Proficient Learning Communities,* or *Inquiry* (2 days f2f)	

Resource D References

Cross, Terry L., Bazron, Barbara J., Dennis, Karl W., & Isaacs, Mareasa R. (1989). *Toward a culturally competent system of care*. Washington, DC: Georgetown University Child Development Program, Child and Adolescent Service System Program.

Dilts, Robert. (1990). *Changing belief systems with NLP*. Capitola, CA: Meta Publications.

Dilts, Robert. (1994). *Effective presentation skills*. Capitola, CA.: Meta.

Fullan, Michael. (2011). *Change leader: Learning to do what matters most*. San Francisco: Jossey-Bass.

Garmston, Robert J., & Wellman, Bruce, M. (1999). *The adaptive school: A sourcebook for developing collaborative groups*. Norwood, MA: Christopher-Gordon Publishers, Inc.

Hargreaves, Andy, & Fullan, Michael. (2012). *Professional capital: Transforming teaching in every school*. New York: Teachers College Press.

Lindsey, Randall B., Nuri Robins, Kikanza, & Terrell, Raymond D. (2009). *Cultural proficiency: A manual for school leaders*, 3rd ed. Thousand Oaks, CA: Corwin.

Senge, Peter M., McCabe, Nelda, Cambron, H., Lucas, Timothy, Kleiner, Art, Dutton, Janis, & Smith, Bryan. (Eds.). (2000). *Schools that learn: A fifth discipline fieldbook for educators, parents, and everyone who cares about education*. New York: Doubleday.

References

Argyris, Chris. (1993). *Knowledge for action: A guide for overcoming barriers to organizational change.* San Francisco: Jossey-Bass.

Cross, Terry L., Bazron, Barbara J., Dennis, Karl W., & Isaacs, Mareasa R. (1989). *Toward a culturally competent system of care.* Washington, DC: Georgetown University Child Development Program, Child and Adolescent Service System Program.

Dilts, Robert. (1990). *Changing belief systems with NLP.* Capitola, CA: Meta.

Dilts, Robert. (1994). *Effective presentation skills.* Capitola, CA: Meta.

Fullan, Michael. (2003). *The moral imperative of school leadership.* Thousand Oaks, CA: Corwin.

Fullan, Michael. (2011). *Change leader: Learning to do what matters most.* San Francisco: Jossey-Bass.

Garmston, Robert J., & Wellman, Bruce, M. (1999). *The adaptive school: A sourcebook for developing collaborative groups.* Norwood, MA: Christopher-Gordon.

Hargreaves, Andy, & Fullan, Michael. (2012). *Professional capital: Transforming teaching in every school.* New York: Teachers College Press.

Hersey, Paul. (1984). *The situational leader.* Escondido, CA: Center for Leadership Studies.

Lindsey, Delores B., Martinez, Richard S., & Lindsey, Randall B. (2009). *Culturally proficient coaching: Supporting educators to create equitable schools.* Thousand Oaks, CA: Corwin.

Lindsey, Delores B., & Lindsey, Randall B. (2014, November/December). Cultural proficiency: Why ask why? *Leadership, 44*(2), 24–27 & 37.

Lindsey, Delores B., Kearney, Karen M., Estrada, Delia, Terrell, Raymond D., & Lindsey, Randall B. (2015). *A culturally proficient response to the common core: Ensuring equity through professional learning.* Thousand Oaks, CA: Corwin.

Lindsey, Randall B., Nuri Robins, Kikanza, & Terrell, Raymond D. (2009). *Cultural proficiency: A manual for school leaders,* 3rd ed. Thousand Oaks, CA: Corwin.

Liswood, Laura. (2010). *The loudest duck: Moving beyond diversity while embracing differences to achieve success at work.* Hoboken, NJ: John Wiley & Sons.

Luft, Joseph, & Ingham, Harrington. (1955). The Johari window, a graphic model of interpersonal awareness. *Proceedings of the western training laboratory in group development.* Los Angeles: UCLA.

McIntosh, Peggy. (1988). *White privilege and male privilege: A personal account of coming to see correspondences through work in women's studies.* MA: Wellesley College.

Senge, Peter M., McCabe, Nelda, Cambron, H., Lucas, Timothy, Kleiner, Art, Dutton, Janis, & Smith, Bryan. (Eds.). (2000). *Schools that learn: A fifth discipline fieldbook for educators, parents, and everyone who cares about education.* New York: Doubleday.

Sinek, Simon. (2009). *Start with why.* New York: The Penguin Group.

Terrell, Raymond D., & Lindsey, Randall B. (2009). *Culturally proficient leadership: The personal journey begins within.* Thousand Oaks, CA: Corwin.

Terrell, Raymond D., & Lindsey, Randall B. (2015). Culturally proficient leadership: Doing what's right for students—all students. In Portelli, John P., & Griffiths, Darrin (Eds.), *Key questions for educational leaders.* Burlington, ON: Word & Deeds.

Index

A SAGE Company

Solutions you want. Experts you trust. Results you need.